# Woods and Forests

# Woods and Forests

## PATRICIA A. FINK MARTIN

**FRANKLIN WATTS**

*A Division of Grolier Publishing*

New York   London   Hong Kong   Sydney

Danbury, Connecticut

*To my family*

**Note to Readers:** Terms defined in glossary are **bold** in the text. In most cases, measurements are given in both metric and English units. Wherever measurements are given in only one system, the units provided are the most appropriate for that situation.

Photographs ©: Donald J. Leopold: cover; Peter Arnold Inc.: 68 (Jeff & Alexa Henry), 32 (Alfred Pasieka); Photo Researchers: 92 (Michael P. Gadomski), 86 (Jim W. Grace), 53 (Omikron), 78 (Rod Planck), 55, 84 (Gregory K. Scott), 30 (Alvin E. Staffan), 70 (L. West); Visuals Unlimited: 24 (R. Calentine), 65 (Steve Maslowski), 74 (Diane R. Nelson), 13 (Dick Poe), 94 (Leonard Lee Rue III), 29 (David Sieren), 12 (John Sohlden).

Diagrams by Bob Italiano, spot art by Steve Savage
Book interior design and pagination by Carole Desnoes

Visit  Franklin Watts on the Internet at:
http://publishing.grolier.com

Library of Congress Cataloging-in-Publication Data

Martin, Patricia A. Fink, 1955–
   Woods and forests / Patricia A. Fink Martin.
      p.  cm. — (Exploring ecosystems)
   Includes bibliographical references and index.
   Summary: Provides instructions for projects and activities that explore forest habitats and demonstrate why they are valuable.
   ISBN 0-531-11697-2 (lib. bdg.)      0-531-16459-4 (pbk.)
   1. Forest ecology—Study and teaching—Activity programs Juvenile literature. [1. Forest ecology—Experiments. 2. Ecology—Experiments. 3. Experiments.] I. Title. II. Series.
QK938.F6M335  2000
577.3'—dc21                                   99-33044
                                           CIP

# Contents

# Woods and Forests

# Introduction

CAN YOU IMAGINE A FOREST WITHOUT its trees? Probably not! After all, trees are the most prominent members of a forest. The coastal redwoods of northern California tower as high as a 35-story building. The wood from a single giant sequoia can weigh as much as 600 tons. No animal is as tall as a redwood or as heavy as a giant sequoia.

Unlike most animals, trees stand rooted to the ground. They are unable to move, except by growth. Still, trees can do some pretty amazing things. Although they have no muscles, they can split apart large boulders and pull water out of the soil. Some can transport water hundreds of feet above the ground. Like other plants, trees make sugars from such simple chemicals as water and carbon dioxide.

The wonder of a forest extends well beyond the majesty of its trees. The woods are home to an amazing variety of living things. Flitting among the leaves and branches, woodland birds enliven forests with splashes of color and cheerful melodies. Hordes of insects chomp, chew, shred, and bore their way through leaves and wood. Squirrels scuttle up and down tree trunks in their daily search for food and safety. Deer roam the woods, browsing on grasses, bushes, and low-lying tree branches.

On the forest floor, salamanders seek the moist coolness under fallen logs and rocky ledges. Spiders crawl through the leaves. Even the soil is teeming with life. It is home to fungi, bacteria, and other tiny creatures.

At one time, forests covered more than one-half of Earth's land surfaces. Today they make up less than one-third of our planet's landscape. Variations in climate and soils have produced five major kinds of forests. They are tropical rain forests, tropical seasonal forests, temperate **deciduous** forests, temperate evergreen forests, and boreal forests. Tropical forests are found near the equator. They are characterized by uniformly warm temperatures throughout the year. Temperate forests, in contrast, exhibit marked seasonal changes. They have cold winters and warm or hot summers. Boreal forests, also called taiga, grow in cold climates with cool, short summers.

North America does not support any tropical forests, but it does have regions covered with temperate deciduous forests, temperate evergreen forests, and boreal forests. This book focuses on these three kinds of forests.

Boreal forests span the width and length of Canada and the northern United States. The most common trees in this vast wilderness are spruce and balsam firs. Areas of temperate deciduous forests are sprinkled across the central and eastern part of the United States. These forests contain maples, beeches, oaks, and hickories. Temperate evergreen forests are found in several parts of North America. The sandy coastal plains of the southeastern and gulf coasts support southeastern scrub pine forests. The western United States is home to one of our most magnificent evergreen forests—the Pacific coastal forest. These forests include some of the world's oldest, largest, and tallest trees. Also in the West, on the slopes of the Rocky Mountains, is a forest of pines, spruces, and firs.

## Two Kinds of Forests

Many scientists divide the forests of North America into two major groups—**coniferous** forests (boreal forests and temperate evergreen forests) and deciduous forests (temperate deciduous forests). What distinguishes these two forest types? The trees.

Cone-bearing trees, or conifers, possess fine, needle-shaped leaves. Conifers replace their leaves a few at a time, but always retain a full **crown** of green. That is why they are sometimes called evergreens. Deciduous trees, such as oaks, birches, hickories, aspens, and maples, unfold broad, flat leaves in the spring and shed them in the autumn.

As you hike through each kind of forest, you will notice other differences, too. Even blindfolded, you can tell the difference between the two kinds of forests. The distinct scent of conifers pervades a coniferous forest. A thick carpet of fallen needles covers the floor, muffling your footsteps. The air is still—you can scarcely feel a breeze on your cheeks. In the hot summer months, the forest feels cool. In the winter, the trees block the chilling winds and provide some protection from the cold.

Winter or summer, the light is dim in a coniferous forest because sunlight barely penetrates the dense screen of needles. Various shades of brown color the forest floor, brightened occasionally by a cluster of ferns or a clump of mosses.

By contrast, a deciduous forest is alive with sound and color during most of the year. In the early spring, clumps of wildflowers dot the forest floor. Later, shrubs burst into bloom and trees unfurl their tender young leaves. In a hike through these woods, you might hear rustling leaves and feel the wind on your face. The sun penetrates this forest more readily, entering through gaps left by fallen trees. Autumn is marked by a final burst of color. Then, a fresh carpet of dead leaves settles upon the forest floor.

In North America, evergreens are most often found in colder climates or in hot, dry areas where sandy soils dominate. The needle-shaped leaves are an adaptation to these conditions.

*Deciduous trees have broad leaves that fall to the ground each autumn.*

## The Forest: Layer by Layer

In every forest, trees share their space with a variety of other green plants, such as mosses, ferns, wildflowers, and shrubs. Scientists describe a forest in terms of the vertical layers created by these different plant types. See Figure 1.

The **canopy,** or overstory, is the highest layer. Here the leafy branches and twigs of the tallest trees bask in the sunlight while shading everything below. Smaller trees make up the next layer, called the **understory.** In

**Figure 1**  Layers of a Deciduous North American Forest

this layer, young saplings compete for a place in the canopy. Smaller trees, such as flowering dogwood, redbud, and sassafras, remain permanent members of the understory.

Shrubs—woody plants with several stems—are often found below the understory. These plants may create a dense thicket that reaches no more than 2 meters (6 ft.) above the ground. An herb layer of ferns, grasses, and wildflowers grows close to the forest floor. Hugging the soil is a ground layer of mosses, lichens, and liverworts. You may not see all these layers in the forests you explore, but every forest has a canopy.

## A Forest's Life

A walk in the woods gives you only a glimpse into the nature of a forest. A forest doesn't pop up overnight, and once present, it seldom stays the same. During its development, a forest goes through many changes. Scientists refer to these changes as **succession.**

A forest may begin as an abandoned field. Soon weedy plants start to grow. Within a few years, this **pioneer community** is gradually replaced by tall grasses and occasional shrubs and tree seedlings. This meadow stage may last for 10 to 20 years. A stage dominated by shrubs follows. It generally remains for 15 to 20 years. In areas where farmland has been abandoned, the maturing forest may skip the shrub stage. Instead, tree seedlings begin to appear in the meadow. These seedlings are fast-growing and sun-loving trees, such as pines. As they grow tall and shade the ground, the meadow becomes a young forest.

Below the larger trees, other young trees begin to sprout up. These new seedlings—oaks, beeches, hickories, and maples—grow slowly in the dense shade. When older trees die and fall over, the younger trees are exposed to more sunlight, and grow quickly to fill in the gap in the canopy. Over a period of 100 years or more, the pine forest transforms into a deciduous forest of long-lived trees.

Unless disturbed, this forest will remain the dominant plant community, or **climax community,** for some time.

## Starting Your Adventure

Come lose yourself in the forest—without getting lost! Grab your walking shoes or hiking boots and enter one of the world's most complex **ecosystems.** Use the activities described in this book to explore this special world. Listen to the sounds of a dead log. Go bear hunting with a microscope. Sharpen your sleuthing skills as you search for secretive woodland mammals. Discover the hidden battles of the forest, where chemical warfare is commonplace! Dare to be an adventurer. Look for the unexpected around the next bend, under a leaf on the forest floor, high above your head, or tucked in a tiny crevice on a tree trunk.

## Safety Tips and Forest Ethics

A trip to the woods can be an exciting adventure—one that's probably even safer than a trip to your local mall! Play it safe, though, and keep the following guidelines in mind.

1. Never venture into the woods alone. Make sure a responsible adult knows where you're going and when you plan to return.
2. Find out if hunting is allowed in the area you'll be exploring. Plan your trips during times when few hunters will be out.
3. Wear shoes that support your ankles and give firm footing on trails.
4. Don't wander off marked paths or take shortcuts, especially on steep slopes. This can result in soil compaction and increased soil erosion.
5. Study a map of the hiking trail before you enter the

forest, and be sure to take a compass. Learn how to use it before your trip!

6. If you do get lost in the woods, stay put! Sit down, rest, or eat a snack. Someone will notice your absence when you don't return on schedule. Searchers have an easier time finding you if you're not moving around.

7. Don't eat or drink anything you find in the woods. Carry your own drinking water and any food you might want during your hike.

8. Obtain permission from landowners to walk across their property.

9. Find out what poisonous plants and snakes live in the area where you'll be hiking. Learn to identify them on sight. Stay away from poison ivy, poison oak, and poison sumac. If you do brush up against any of these plants, wash the area of skin that touched the poisonous plant thoroughly with soap and water as soon as you get home!

10. Ticks can be abundant in some woods in the warmer months. Because some ticks carry diseases, such as Lyme disease, it's important to check yourself thoroughly when you leave the woods. If you notice a bull's-eye skin rash around a tick bite, see a doctor immediately!

11. Watch your step as you hike. Trails are never as smooth as paved walkways. Roots, rocks, and fallen logs can trip you up. Step over, not on, loose rocks and logs.

12. Pack out everything you carry in. Don't leave trash or litter behind!

## Keeping Track

Keeping a journal of your experiences is easy and can be quite rewarding. All you need is a bound notebook and a pencil or a pen with waterproof ink. Choose a notebook large enough to allow for sketches and notes, but small enough to easily fit into a backpack or fanny-pack. Because rain is common in any forest, keep your notebook in a large resealable plastic bag or purchase a notebook made of water-resistant paper.

Use your journal to record your observations and any questions that come to you while you're exploring. Don't think you'll remember everything when you get back home! It's easy to forget the details, so write them down while they are fresh in your mind. Even if you think you can't draw, include sketches of what you see.

You might want to include some of the following data in your journal:

- date, time, location
- weather conditions (temperature, wind direction and speed, relative humidity, cloud conditions)
- plant-life observations (types, numbers, descriptions)
- animal-life observations (types, numbers, distribution, behaviors, adaptations)
- surrounding area (land-use patterns; special features, odors)
- soil conditions (water saturation, soil type, erosion)
- anything that seems special or unusual

While your field journal is your most important piece of equipment, some of the activities in this book call for other kinds of equipment. You will find directions for constructing these devices in the Appendix at the back of this book.

# CHAPTER 1

# Giants of the Plant Kingdom: The Wonder of Trees

IT WAS THE HIKERS' FIRST VISIT TO the Great Smoky Mountains National Park. With guidebooks in hand and binoculars hung around their necks, the group set out in search of nature's wonders. The hikers oohed and aahed over spectacular waterfalls and clear, rushing streams. They congratulated themselves on spotting rare and beautiful birds and marveled at the showy wildflowers that covered the forest floor. They walked down miles of hiking trails, striding past trunk after trunk of the ruling members of the forest. Yet not once did they stop and appreciate these forest giants.

For most of us, trees are commonplace. We seldom count them among nature's wonders. Yet they are the tallest and heaviest living things on Earth. They protect the soil, keep our water clean, and

19

provide a habitat and food for many living creatures. Trees also produce wood—an amazing substance of great strength and resilience. Wood is tough and long lasting yet completely biodegradable.

Unlike other woody plants, most of a tree's wood is in the form of a single, straight trunk. The trunk supports a leafy crown of branches, twigs, and leaves that rises up to 111 meters (365 ft.) above the ground. This lofty height gives the food-producing leaves an advantage over other plants—ready access to plenty of sunlight. Anchoring a tree's crown and trunk to the soil are its roots. The roots also extract water and essential minerals from the soil.

Internal systems of tiny tubes link the leaves, trunk, and roots. One set of tubes, the **xylem,** transports water and dissolved minerals from the roots up into the crown of the tree. The second set, the **phloem,** carries food (sugars) from the leaves to other parts of the tree.

Most of the food carried by the phloem is transported to the tree's growth zones. Trees grow at the tips of their roots, just underneath the bark, and at the **buds** on their twigs. Unlike most animals, plants keep growing even after they're mature.

There's so much about trees that escapes our notice. Use the activities in this chapter to get to know these often-ignored giants of the plant world.

**INVESTIGATION 1**

## What Can You See in a Block of Wood?

No matter where you are, chances are that something made of wood is close at hand. Look carefully at its surface. What do you see? Probably not much beyond the patterns of dark lines or grain.

This is your chance to examine the detailed structure of wood. Start your investigation with a piece of balsa wood.

Balsa is a **hardwood** tree with very soft wood. Hobby shops often carry balsa wood because people use it to build models.

Buy a piece that measures 1 × 1 centimeter (0.4 × 0.4 in.), with a minimum length of 10 centimeters (4 in.). If you can't find balsa wood, look for basswood, or pick up twigs from willows or poplars. Collect a cutting board, forceps, a pack of single-edged razor blades, your journal, and a hand lens. Better yet, borrow a dissecting microscope from your school's science department.

Place your wood sample on the cutting board. Using a fresh single-edged razor blade, carefully shave off a very thin cross section perpendicular to the long axis. See Figure 2a on the next page. *Watch your fingers as you work!* Make a few thin cuts, then choose your best cross section to view under magnification.

Examine the section with a hand lens or dissecting microscope. Do you see the large holes in the wood? They are sections of long, tubular cells called **vessel elements.** Vessel elements are stacked end to end, from the root tips up to each leaf of the tree, to form vessels. Vessels are part of the xylem tissue that transports water and dissolved substances. You can also see much smaller holes in the wood. These are sections of fibers that give wood its strength.

Other cell types can be seen by shaving thin longitudinal sections, about 1 centimeter (0.4 in.) in length, off adjacent sides of the wood stick. First, shave off a few longitudinal slices from one side of the wood stick. See Figure 2b. Support the wood against the cutting board as you cut.

Rotate the stick one-quarter turn and make a few more thin longitudinal slices along the face adjacent to the one you just finished cutting. See Figure 2c.

You'll notice that the sections cut from adjacent faces of the wood stick look different. Some will have clusters of dark brown lines that run from side to side. The structures you see in these radial sections are called **rays.** Rays are bands of small cells that radiate out from the center of the tree trunk. They form pathways for the movement of food and water. A radial section provides a side view of these cells.

**Figure 2**   Viewing the Structure of Wood

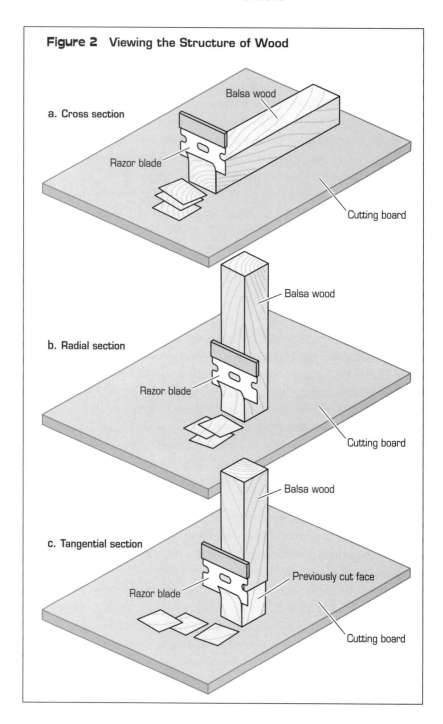

a. Cross section

Balsa wood

Razor blade

Cutting board

b. Radial section

Balsa wood

Razor blade

Cutting board

c. Tangential section

Balsa wood

Razor blade

Previously cut face

Cutting board

In sections cut from the adjacent face of the wood stick, look for thin, dark brown streaks that run up and down. Here you are viewing wood as it might be seen in a scraping just inside the bark of an intact tree trunk. This is a tangential section. The dark brown streaks are rays viewed at their ends as they radiate out from the center of the trunk. Fibers may appear at the very edges of the section as light-colored stringy-looking material. You may also see vessels running the length of the section.

### ✔ Doing More

Try cutting sections of other types of wood. Compare the wood of **softwoods**, such as pine or fir, to balsa wood. How do they differ?

**INVESTIGATION 2**

# History Written on a Stump

Archaeologists have long puzzled over lost civilizations—people and cultures that vanished without a trace. At one time, the disappearance of the cliff dwellers of Mesa Verde or the Lost Colony of Roanoke Island seemed to be unsolvable mysteries lost to the past. Recently, though, scientists have discovered some clues. The clues weren't found in pieces of pottery or stone drawings. They were hidden in the trees.

Trees hold records of past climatic events in their wood. Based on studies of the wood of local trees, scientists think that severe droughts drove the cliff dwellers and the colonists away from their homes.

What clues to the past can you see in a tree stump? To learn to read what's written in the wood, collect the following items: a small ruler, a pencil, notebook paper, pushpins, scrap pine lumber, a hand lens, your journal, and fireplace logs or sections of tree trunks. Check your school's science department or a local nature museum for tree sections or

*Can you count the growth rings on this white oak stump?*

"rounds" that you can borrow. A tree service might cut you a section for free. You could also make a trip to nearby woods to look for tree stumps.

Select a tree stump or tree round with obvious alternating rings of light and dark wood. Use your hand lens to get a closer look. In the spring, when water is plentiful, a tree produces wood with large cells. These cells form light-colored bands. The wood produced later in the growing season contains smaller cells with thick cell walls. They form dark bands of wood. As a result, each year's growth, or **annual ring,** consists of an inner circle of lighter wood and an outer circle of darker wood. The lighter wood is sometimes called early, or spring, wood, while the darker wood is referred to as late, or summer, wood.

Now count the annual rings. If the section was cut from the base of the tree, counting the rings will tell you how old the tree is. Lay a sheet of notebook paper over half of the stump or section so the edge of paper passes through the center. Hold the paper in place with pushpins. Beginning in the center of the wood, count outward and mark the paper's edge each time it crosses an annual ring. If the rings are close together, use a hand lens to get a better view. How many rings did you count?

These rings hold many clues to the past—indications of fires, drought, insect attacks, abundant rainfall, and competition from neighboring trees. A blackened area within the rings is evidence of a fire. Very narrow rings might indicate years of drought, insect attacks, or crowding. Wide rings appear during years of plentiful rain and good growing conditions. What stories can you read in the wood?

### ✔ Doing More

Compare a section of a forest tree with a piece of pine lumber. Look for a board cut from the middle of a log, so that even the earliest years of growth can be seen. Count the number of annual rings in 5 to 10 centimeters (2 to 4 in.) of wood. To calculate an average growth rate per year, divide the width of wood examined by the number of annual rings. A phenomenal growth rate of 2.5 centimeters (1 in.) per year was recorded for a tree grown on an Alabama tree farm. What growth rates are exhibited in your wood samples?

# A Closer Look at Twigs

During a single year, a large oak tree might grow hundreds of feet into the air. To measure this incredible growth, examine the twigs. It is here, among hundreds or thousands of tiny fingers, that such growth occurs.

How much does each twig grow? Which twigs grow the most? To answer these questions and a few more that might surprise you, collect an old pair of scissors or pruning shears, ribbon or strips of fabric, a small ruler, a hand lens, plastic bags, a throw rope, masking tape, a field guide to trees, your journal, and a permanent marker. The Appendix at the back of this book has instructions for making a throw rope.

Take a stroll around your neighborhood or a local park to collect twigs. Winter is the best time of year for this activity, but you can also try it during fall and summer. Gather six to ten twigs from at least three different kinds of deciduous trees. Be sure to ask permission before collecting twigs from a neighbor's tree! Clip only healthy twigs. Flick the bark with your thumbnail to see the wood underneath—a live twig will reveal green wood.

Use the throw rope to get twigs just out of your reach. With scissors or pruning shears, make a clean cut 20 to 30 centimeters (8 to 12 in.) from the tip of each twig. Number each twig with masking tape. Record the location and date in your journal, and use the field guide to identify each tree.

Study your twigs on a table with good overhead lighting. Using a hand lens, carefully examine each twig from the tip to the base. You may see a terminal bud, lateral buds, terminal bud scales, terminal bud scale scars, and leaf scars. Use Figure 3 to help you identify these features.

Can you tell how old each twig is? Look for changes in bark color along the length of a twig. Where the bark changes color you'll see several tiny lines very close together. This is the site where the previous year's terminal bud grew. During the winter, it was protected with tough outer sheaths, or

**Figure 3**   Features of a Twig

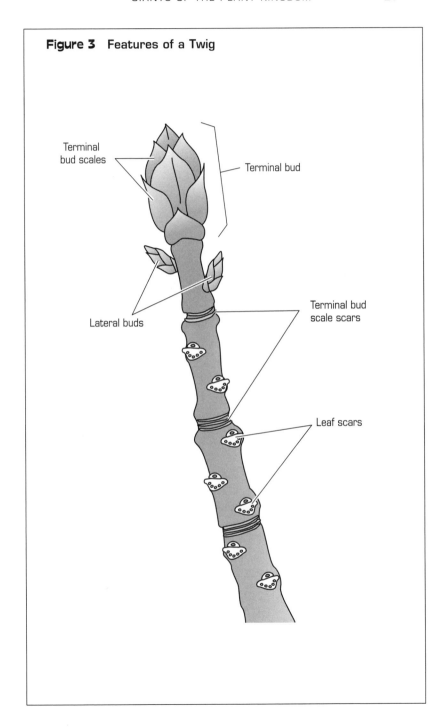

scales. When growth resumed in the spring, the scales fell off, leaving these tiny scars on the bark. To learn the age of a twig, count the clusters of terminal bud scale scars, starting from the tip of the twig.

To determine annual growth rates, measure the distance between groups of scale scars. Record this information in your journal. If you have several twigs from the same tree, compare growth rates of similar years. Do they differ? If so, can you think of why?

On a tree that's close to home, follow the current year's growth from early spring to fall. Measure and record the growth of several twigs weekly. Use ribbon or flagging to mark the twigs you are monitoring. When is the period of most rapid growth?

### ✔ Doing More

Impress your friends and family by learning to identify trees in winter—just by looking at their twigs. Twig characteristics are unique to each tree species. You'll need a hand lens and an identification guide, or **key,** to twigs in your region. For references, check the For Further Information section at the back of this book.

# Tree Beginnings

Trees are amazing growers. From seeds the size of your thumbnail or smaller grow some of the most massive living things on Earth. If you plant a young seedling today, it will soon tower over your head, and it will continue to grow even after you are long gone. If you chop the tree down, it may still grow—from sprouts that come up from the roots.

Plant a tree seed and watch its amazing growth, day by day. You'll need tree seeds; 6- or 8-inch (15- or 20-cm) pots; potting soil; a shovel; a meterstick; a pencil; your journal;

small plastic bags; sand, peat moss, or vermiculite; a tree identification guide; and a refrigerator.

Collect seeds from trees in your neighborhood or a local park. The seeds of many deciduous trees can be found in the fall, when they mature and fall to the ground. The winged seeds of maples or ashes, pods of locusts, sweetgum balls, acorns, or nuts of hickory or walnut trees are easy to spot. While most seeds mature in the fall, some ripen in late spring. Look for the seeds of elms, cottonwoods, willows, and red maples at this time. Use a field guide to trees to identify the seeds you've collected.

You may have a supply of seeds as close as your refrigerator or kitchen counter. Apples, grapefruits, and oranges contain seeds that will readily grow. If no fruit seeds are available, you can order seeds by mail. (See the For Further Information section at the back of this book for a list of nurseries and seed companies.) Be sure to purchase seeds suitable for the climate in your area.

*Double-winged fruits of a maple tree*

*Acorns of a chinkadin oak*

Before most tree seeds will grow, they need to be exposed to cold temperatures for a period of time. You can plant your seeds outdoors in the fall to expose them to winter conditions, or create an artificial winter by placing the seeds in your refrigerator. This seed pretreatment process is called **stratification.** Mix a few seeds with two or three handfuls of moistened sand, peat moss, or vermiculite. Seal the mixture in a plastic bag, and place it in your refrigerator for at least 8 weeks.

If you've purchased tree seeds from a supplier, follow their directions for pretreatment. Seeds from citrus fruits like oranges and grapefruits can be planted directly, but apple seeds will need to be stratified.

To plant your seeds, fill several pots with potting soil. Push seeds the size of your thumbnail or larger about 5 to 8 centimeters (2 to 3 in.) into the soil. Smaller seeds should be planted 1 to 3 centimeters ( $\frac{1}{2}$ to 1 in.) below the surface. Top with a layer of loose soil. Moisten the soil with water and place the pots in a sunny area. Keep the soil moist until the seeds have germinated. Germination rates vary. Citrus seeds will **germinate** in 10 to 15 days, while others may take 30 days or longer.

If several seeds in the same pot sprout, separate them and replant them in individual pots or in the ground. When transplanting, use a pencil to lift the seedling out of the dirt. Monitor shoot heights daily.

### ✔ Doing More

Many deciduous trees and some conifers produce sprouts from roots. In your visits to the woods, look for root sprouts growing at the base of oak, black locust, sweetgum, or tulip poplar stumps.

# Leaky Leaves:
# Measuring Rates of Transpiration

Everyone knows that plants need water. Trees need lots of water. An oak tree may consume 570 liters (150 gal.) on a hot summer day. On a similar day, a birch could take up more than 1,500 liters (400 gal.) of water! Most of that water will evaporate. It is lost through tiny pores, or **stomata,** in the surfaces of leaves. This process of water loss from leaves is called **transpiration.**

You can measure this water loss using a simple device made from 1 meter (3.3 feet) of standard airline aquarium tubing. You'll also need a waterproof marker, graph paper, a ruler, pruning shears or scissors, a cup, tape, a thermometer, your journal, and a flat, vertical surface to use as a support. A bulletin board, plywood, or foam board will work.

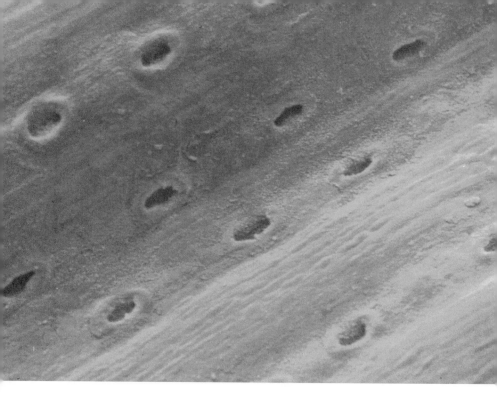

*This scanning electron micrograph (SEM) reveals small pits dotting the surface of a pine needle. At the base of each pit lies a stoma, a tiny opening in the needle's epidermis through which gases pass.*

Fill a cup with water, grab your pruning shears or scissors, and head outside to the nearest tree. Scan the crown for twigs with green leaves. Once you've found one, clip a 15-centimeter (6-in.) length. Immediately place the cut end in water and carry the twig indoors.

Find an area next to a window where you can work. Prop your board upright on a chair or table. Cut a 1-meter (3.3-ft.) section of tubing. Fill the tubing with water from a faucet. Flush out any air bubbles in the line. Holding the two cut ends upright, carry the tubing over to your support board. Form the tubing into a U shape with both ends level. Secure the tubing to the vertical support with tape. See Figure 4.

Remove the leaves from the bottom 3 to 5 centimeters (1 to 2 in.) of the twig. Take the twig out of the cup, and push it into one end of the tubing until the stripped portion is im-

**Figure 4** Measuring Transpiration

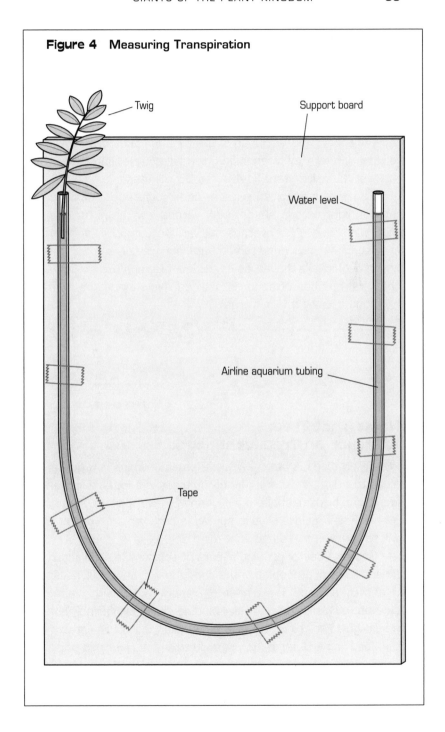

Twig

Support board

Water level

Airline aquarium tubing

Tape

mersed in water. Mark the water level of the other end of the tubing with a permanent marker. Set a thermometer nearby and note the time and temperature in your journal. At the end of 30 minutes, measure the distance the water level has dropped from the marked line. Divide that distance by the number of minutes elapsed. This is the transpiration rate. Be sure to record a description of the lighting conditions in your journal. Under most conditions, the water level should drop at least 10 millimeters (0.4 in.) in 30 minutes.

Compare transpiration rates under different conditions: intense light versus shade; high versus low temperatures; high wind (use a fan) versus still air. To compare different tree species, you'll need to estimate leaf area. Trace the outline of each twig's the leaves on a sheet of graph paper. Count the total number of squares outlined. Now divide the transpiration rate by the leaf area.

# Name That Tree:
# A Primer on Tree Identification

Identifying trees is like a detective game in which you gather clues to solve a mystery. Identifying trees is a lot easier than identifying birds because a tree won't fly away just as you pull out your field guide. Unless someone cuts the tree down, it will be there in the same spot for many years to come.

Gather a pair of pruning shears or scissors, a highlighter, a hand lens, photocopies of the data sheets shown in Figures 5 and 6, a three-ring binder or report folder with plastic sleeves, a ruler, a large metal binding clip, your journal, and a field guide to trees. Several good field guides are listed in the For Further Information section at the back of this book. Bring along binoculars and a throw rope to help you gather leaves. You can make a throw rope using the instructions in the Appendix at the back of this book.

**Figure 5 Data Sheet of the Characteristics of Broad-leaved (Deciduous) Trees**

Name of Observer _____  Tree Location _____  Habitat Type _____

Date _____  Approximate Height _____

*Leaves*
Size of Leaves _____

**Types of Leaves**
☐ Simple
☐ Compound
  ☐ Palmate
  ☐ Pinnate
  ☐ Bipinnate

**Arrangement of Leaves**
☐ Opposite
☐ Alternate
☐ Whorled

**Shape of Leaves**
☐ No lobes
☐ Rounded lobes
☐ Pointed lobes
☐ Heart shaped
☐ Narrow

**Edges of Leaves**
☐ Smooth
☐ Toothed
☐ Double toothed

*Trunk and Branches*
Color of Bark _____

**Texture of Bark**
☐ Smooth
☐ Papery
☐ Rough

**Pattern of Bark**
☐ Diamond
☐ Horizontal
☐ Vertical

**Thorns**
☐ Present
☐ Absent

*Flowers*
Size of flowers _____
Color of flowers _____
Number of petals _____
Date of blossoms _____

*Seeds/Fruits*
Description _____
_____
_____
_____
_____
_____
_____

*Shape of Tree*
(Draw a picture)

*Name of Tree*
(Use the information on this sheet and a field guide.)

# Figure 6 Data Sheet of the Characteristics of Needle-leaved (Coniferous) Trees

Name of Observer _____ Tree Location _____ Habitat Type _____

Date _____ Approximate Height _____

**Needles**

Size of Needles _____

**Arrangement of Needles**
- [ ] One needle/cluster
- [ ] Two needles/cluster
- [ ] Three needles/cluster
- [ ] Five needles/cluster
- [ ] More than five needles/cluster

**Shape of Needles**
- [ ] Square
- [ ] Round
- [ ] Triangular
- [ ] Flat

**Color of Needles**
- [ ] Green
- [ ] Blue-green
- [ ] Two white stripes on bottom

**Berries**

Size of Berries _____

Shape of Berries _____

Color of Berries _____

**Trunk**

Color of Bark _____

**Texture of Bark**
- [ ] Smooth
- [ ] Rough
- [ ] Resin blisters

**Branches**
- [ ] Droop
- [ ] Look like flat layers

**Twigs**
- [ ] Deeply grooved
- [ ] Small woody pegs
- [ ] Knobbles and warty spurs
- [ ] Hairy
- [ ] Covered with white powder

**Cones**

Size of Cones _____

**Shape of Cones**
- [ ] Spherical
- [ ] Short, oval
- [ ] Long, tapered

**Shape of Scales**
- [ ] Pointed
- [ ] Rounded

**Orientation on Twig**
- [ ] Upright
- [ ] Hanging

*Shape of Tree*
[Draw a picture]

*Name of Tree*
[Use the information on this sheet and a field guide.]

The best time to do this activity is in late spring or summer. Begin by studying a tree in your yard or neighborhood. Does the tree have needle-shaped leaves or broad, flat leaves? If it's a broad-leaved tree, notice the arrangement of leaves along a twig. Are they directly opposite one another or do they alternate? Next, look at the form of the leaves. Are they divided into small leaflets? Figure 7 will help you identify leaf types.

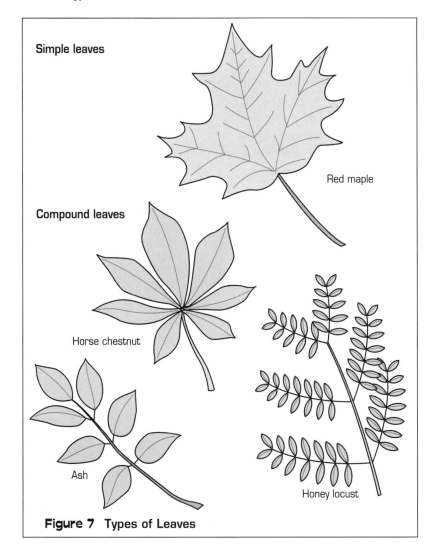

**Simple leaves**

Red maple

**Compound leaves**

Horse chestnut

Ash

Honey locust

**Figure 7** Types of Leaves

Using either Figure 5 or Figure 6 as a guide, collect as much information as you can about the tree. Gather a few leaves, twigs, seeds, cones, or flowers to examine up close. If some of the leaves look different from the others, take samples of each type. Scan higher in the tree with your binoculars. Look for clues on the ground too, but keep in mind that these clues aren't as reliable!

Store your evidence in plastic sleeves in the three-ring binder for future study. Label each sleeve with a number that corresponds to the number you've placed on the data sheet. Use the metal binding clip to close the open end of the plastic sleeves.

Once you've completed your data sheet, consult a field guide to make the final identification. As a beginner, you may wish to focus on major tree families or groups. Later you can start learning tree species.

Some trees are not so easy to identify. After all, not every tree is the perfect example of its species. Some trees may show only a few of the features listed in your field guide. Some trees, especially oaks, readily form **hybrids.** A hybrid is the offspring of parents of two different varieties or two different species. This makes identification even more difficult!

# CHAPTER 2

# Bathed by the Air and Rooted in the Soil: Trees and Their Environment

PICTURE YOURSELF STANDING IN THE middle of a baseball field, right on top of the pitcher's mound. It's the middle of August. The hot summer sun is high in the sky, burning straight down on you. You wish you'd brought a cap or sunglasses, but you have neither.

The sun and the heat are almost unbearable. To make matters worse, a dry, hot wind has started to blow, kicking up clouds of dust. The dust swirls your way. Coughing, you bend to the ground and hide your face in your hands. The ground beneath you is hard and dry.

Years ago, a forest grew in this very spot. The soil was spongy and moist. A thick layer of leaves and fallen branches carpeted the forest floor. The sunlight barely penetrated the dense forest canopy. The air felt still and cool.

What a difference a few trees can make! Even a single tree changes its immediate surroundings, or its "microenvironment." Trees create their own weather, or "microclimate," by altering temperatures, humidity, and wind speed.

Trees shade the soil and send out countless fingers of roots and delicate root hairs. Root hairs are minute, threadlike extensions of cells on the outer surface of a root. The roots loosen the soil, letting in air and water. Trees drop leaves, twigs, and branches to the ground, returning essential nutrients to the earth. The activities in this chapter will help you explore the special world around a tree.

## Under the Big Green Top: Light Levels from the Top Down

From darkness as black as night to blazing, glaring sunlight, light levels vary greatly in a forest, even on a cloudless summer day. As sunlight penetrates the canopy, millions of leaves deflect and absorb the sun's rays.

To measure light levels in the forest, scientists use a light meter. You can make reasonable estimates, however, with sheets of sun sensitive paper. You'll also need a stopwatch, water, plastic resealable sandwich bags, a permanent marker, your journal, a plastic bowl, and an extendible pole. Instructions for making your own extendible pole are provided in the Appendix at the back of this book.

Sun sensitive papers, such as Solargraphics, are sold at hobby shops and some toy stores. When these papers are exposed to light and developed, they turn blue. Dark blues are the result of high light levels, while paler shades of blue result from lower light levels.

Choose a cloudless sunny day to begin this activity. Find an outdoor area close to your home where you can work. Read the directions that come with the sun sensitive papers. A pack of papers will be wrapped in a black plastic bag. Carefully pull one sheet from the pack without letting sunlight expose the rest of the papers. Place the sheet inside a plastic sandwich bag. This will prevent the paper from being blown by the wind.

Lay the bag in the sun. Leave it there for the time recommended by the manufacturer. Develop the paper with water, and let it dry. Try a few more sheets. Store these papers in a sandwich bag labeled "Full Sunlight." Include the date on the label. Now develop a few sheets that have not been exposed to sunlight. Keep these in a bag labeled "No Sunlight."

To check out light levels in the woods, carry your supplies with you, along with a jug of water and an extendible pole. Expose and develop the sun sensitive papers as described above. Don't vary the exposure time—stick to the same one you used earlier. Compare the colors of these papers to those you developed near your home.

Once you've mastered this technique, compare light levels at the top and bottom of a forest. Use an extendible pole to get above the understory. Find a nearby open field to estimate light levels reaching the top of the forest canopy.

How much do light levels vary within a single layer of the forest? Try exposing papers at various sites on the forest floor. Step off the trail and walk in a straight line through the woods. Stop every three paces to expose and develop a paper. How much variation in color do you see among the papers? During the summer, compare light levels in woods dominated by deciduous trees with those in woods dominated by coniferous trees.

## ✔ Doing More

By using a series of standards—papers exposed to known light levels—and the data you've already collected, you can make more accurate estimates of light levels.

In addition to the supplies listed above, you'll need scissors, shading film, clear acetate film, and graph paper. Shad-

| Table 1 Amount of Sunlight Filtered by Shading Film | |
| --- | --- |
| Kind of Shading Film | Amount of Sunlight Filtered |
| 20 percent<br>40 percent<br>60 percent | 32 to 39 percent<br>50 to 62 percent<br>72 to 78 percent |

ing film and acetate film are available from art and drafting supply stores. Purchase one sheet each of shading film with each of the following shading ranges: 20 percent, 40 percent, and 60 percent. Pull each sheet off its paper backing and stick it onto a sheet of clear acetate. Trim the sheets to the size of the sun sensitive paper.

Now slide a sheet of shading film inside a plastic sandwich bag. Place a sheet of sun sensitive paper underneath the film. Expose it to direct sunlight on a cloudless day. Then develop and dry the paper. Repeat this procedure with the other shading films. After drying, store each paper in a sandwich bag. These sheets will serve as your standards. Use Table 1 to determine the amount of sunlight filtered by each shading film. On each bag, mark that percentage.

Match each paper developed in the woods to the standard closest in color. Read the percent of sunlight off the plastic bags. Construct a table to record this information in your journal. Display some of your data on a graph. For example, plot percent of sunlight on the horizontal axis and height on the vertical axis.

PROJECT **3**

# Weather in the Woods: Taking a Forest's Temperature

Imagine journeying from a cool, still, lush place to one with glaring sun, strong wind, and intense heat—all in a space of

30 meters (100 ft.) or less. Where could you find such differences in weather? In the forest!

You don't need sophisticated equipment to investigate the weather in the woods. Meteorologists sometime use balloons to obtain their data. In this activity, you'll make a weather balloon to take temperature readings in a forest. You'll need a thermometer, 2- to 4-pound test monofilament fishing line, two or more jumbo helium balloons, duct tape, scissors, graph paper, a permanent marker, a measuring tape, and your journal.

Science suppliers usually sell student thermometers—small thermometers attached to thin plastic cards. If you don't want to buy one, borrow one from your science teacher. ***Don't use a mercury thermometer! If broken, it will leak mercury, which is toxic to you and to forest creatures.***

You can purchase helium balloons from a local florist or a party supply store. Balloons will lose their buoyancy within 24 hours, so buy your balloons the day you plan to do the activity. Two large Mylar balloons or two 18-inch nylon balloons will lift a small student thermometer. Buy a few extra balloons just to be sure you have enough lift to take your thermometer up, up, and away!

Place small flags of duct tape every meter along a 30-meter (100-ft.) length of fishing line. With a marker, label the second flag "0." On each of the remaining flags, write the distance from that second flag. Rewind the line when you're done.

Plan a trip to a nearby wooded area with an open field or meadow close by. On a still, calm day, gather your supplies and purchase your balloons. Once you've reached the woods, tie your balloons to a tree limb while you get organized.

When you're ready, tie the balloons together. Make a small loop with the free end of the balloon strings and attach the thermometer to this loop. Tie the fishing line to the loop, so the flag labeled "0" is even with the bulb of the thermometer. To keep the fishing line from slipping, make several tight knots.

Scan the canopy for a good place to let your balloons rise. Slowly release them by letting out the fishing line. Watch out for sharp limbs. To take temperature readings, hold the balloons steady for 5 minutes. Note the height by reading the nearest tape flag on the fishing line. Quickly reel in the line. Without touching the bulb of the thermometer, read and record the temperature. Determine the actual height of the thermometer by adding the length of fishing line released to the height of your hands. Record this information as well as the time of day and the weather conditions in your journal.

Take temperature readings at ground level and at the following heights in meters: 1, 3, 6, 9, 15, and 30. Repeat the same measurements in a nearby open field.

Graph your data. Plot temperature on the horizontal axis and height on the vertical axis. How do the graphs of data from the woods and open field compare?

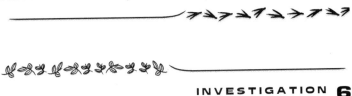

## Leafy Humidifiers

In the course of a day, gallons of water silently and invisibly slip away from the leaves of a tree. Every day, 1 acre of trees releases more than 3,000 gallons of water to the atmosphere (an acre is a little larger than a football field). The water escapes, not as a liquid, but as a gas called water vapor.

You can trap and measure the escaping water vapor with the following supplies: several plastic bread bags, twist ties, safety glasses, a sling psychrometer, a pipette or medicine dropper, distilled water, and your journal. A sling psychrometer is an instrument used to measure humidity. Inexpensive models can be purchased from the science supply companies listed in the For Further Information section at the back of this book.

Try this simple demonstration to see the water released by tree leaves. Locate a large tree near your home. Place a plastic bag around a healthy twig with four or five leaves. Use the twist tie to close the bag's open end tightly around the woody stem. Select three or four other twigs and enclose them in plastic bags, too. Place the last bag around a cluster of dead leaves or on a dead twig. This twig will serve as a **control group**.

Check the bags every hour. If they look cloudy, take a closer look. You'll probably see tiny droplets of water that have condensed on the inside of the bag. Where did this water come from? Examine the control bag. Does it look different from the others? Why or why not?

Water escaping through the leaves affects the humidity of the air. Because the amount of water vapor that air can hold varies with the temperature of the air, scientists express humidity in a special way. The amount of water vapor in the air at a particular temperature on a given day is compared to the amount of water vapor the air can hold at that temperature. This ratio, expressed as a percent, is called **relative humidity**.

Measure relative humidity with a sling psychrometer, a pipette, and a small bottle of distilled water. On a sunny day, visit two sites—a bare field and a wooded area—that you can reach within a short period of time. Record the time of day, type of dominant vegetation, temperature, and sky conditions at each location.

*As you use the sling psychrometer, stand away from people. Hold the thermometers away from your face, and wear safety glasses to protect your eyes. Check that the thermometers are securely fastened to their holder before you start swinging!*

When you're ready to take a reading, add several drops of distilled water to the wick of the wet-bulb thermometer. Holding the psychrometer by the handle, whirl the apparatus for at least 1 minute, until the temperature of the wet-bulb thermometer stops dropping. Immediately read the wet-bulb temperature and record it in your journal. Read the dry-bulb reading and record it.

To determine relative humidity from these readings, use Table 2 on pages 46 and 47. First, find your dry-bulb reading. Next, locate the difference between your wet- and dry-bulb readings. Run your finger from the dry-bulb reading across the row until it intersects the column giving the

## Table 2　How to Find Relative Humidity

Dry-bulb Temperature (°C)

Difference Between Dry-bulb and Wet-bulb Temperatures

| | 0.5 | 1.0 | 1.5 | 2.0 | 2.5 | 3.0 | 3.5 | 4.0 | 4.5 | 5.0 | 5.5 | 6.0 | 6.5 | 7 |
|---|---|---|---|---|---|---|---|---|---|---|---|---|---|---|
| 10 | 94 | 88 | 82 | 77 | 71 | 66 | 60 | 55 | 50 | 44 | 39 | 34 | 29 | 2 |
| 11 | 94 | 89 | 83 | 78 | 72 | 67 | 61 | 56 | 51 | 46 | 41 | 36 | 32 | 2 |
| 12 | 94 | 89 | 83 | 78 | 73 | 68 | 63 | 58 | 53 | 48 | 43 | 39 | 34 | 2 |
| 13 | 95 | 89 | 83 | 79 | 74 | 69 | 64 | 59 | 54 | 50 | 45 | 41 | 36 | 3 |
| 14 | 95 | 90 | 84 | 79 | 75 | 70 | 65 | 60 | 56 | 51 | 47 | 42 | 38 | 3 |
| 15 | 95 | 90 | 85 | 80 | 75 | 71 | 66 | 61 | 57 | 53 | 48 | 44 | 40 | 3 |
| 16 | 95 | 90 | 85 | 81 | 76 | 71 | 67 | 63 | 58 | 54 | 50 | 46 | 42 | 3 |
| 17 | 95 | 90 | 86 | 81 | 76 | 75 | 68 | 64 | 60 | 55 | 51 | 47 | 43 | 4 |
| 18 | 95 | 91 | 86 | 82 | 77 | 73 | 69 | 65 | 61 | 57 | 53 | 49 | 45 | 4 |
| 19 | 95 | 91 | 87 | 82 | 78 | 74 | 70 | 65 | 62 | 58 | 54 | 50 | 46 | 4 |
| 20 | 96 | 91 | 87 | 83 | 78 | 74 | 70 | 66 | 63 | 59 | 55 | 51 | 48 | 4 |
| 21 | 96 | 91 | 87 | 83 | 79 | 75 | 71 | 67 | 64 | 60 | 56 | 53 | 49 | 4 |
| 22 | 96 | 92 | 87 | 83 | 80 | 76 | 72 | 68 | 64 | 61 | 57 | 54 | 50 | 4 |
| 23 | 96 | 92 | 88 | 84 | 80 | 76 | 72 | 69 | 65 | 62 | 58 | 55 | 52 | 4 |
| 24 | 96 | 92 | 88 | 84 | 80 | 77 | 73 | 69 | 66 | 62 | 59 | 56 | 53 | 4 |
| 25 | 96 | 92 | 88 | 84 | 81 | 77 | 74 | 70 | 67 | 63 | 60 | 57 | 54 | 5 |
| 26 | 96 | 92 | 88 | 85 | 81 | 78 | 74 | 71 | 67 | 64 | 61 | 58 | 54 | 5 |
| 27 | 96 | 92 | 89 | 85 | 82 | 78 | 75 | 71 | 68 | 65 | 62 | 58 | 56 | 5 |
| 28 | 96 | 93 | 89 | 85 | 82 | 78 | 75 | 72 | 69 | 65 | 62 | 59 | 56 | 5 |
| 29 | 96 | 93 | 89 | 86 | 82 | 79 | 76 | 72 | 69 | 66 | 63 | 60 | 57 | 5 |
| 30 | 96 | 93 | 89 | 86 | 83 | 79 | 76 | 73 | 70 | 67 | 64 | 61 | 58 | 5 |
| 31 | 96 | 93 | 90 | 86 | 83 | 80 | 77 | 73 | 70 | 67 | 64 | 61 | 59 | 5 |
| 32 | 96 | 93 | 90 | 86 | 83 | 80 | 77 | 74 | 71 | 68 | 65 | 62 | 60 | 5 |
| 33 | 97 | 93 | 90 | 87 | 83 | 80 | 77 | 74 | 71 | 68 | 66 | 63 | 60 | 5 |
| 34 | 97 | 93 | 90 | 87 | 84 | 81 | 78 | 75 | 72 | 69 | 66 | 63 | 61 | 5 |
| 35 | 97 | 94 | 90 | 87 | 84 | 81 | 78 | 75 | 72 | 69 | 67 | 64 | 61 | 5 |

| .5 | 8.0 | 8.5 | 9.0 | 9.5 | 10.0 | 10.5 | 11.0 | 11.5 | 12.0 | 12.5 | 13.0 | 13.5 | 14.0 | 14.5 | 15.0 |
|---|---|---|---|---|---|---|---|---|---|---|---|---|---|---|---|
| 0 | 15 | 10 | 6 |  |  |  |  |  |  |  |  |  |  |  |  |
| 2 | 18 | 13 | 9 | 5 |  |  |  |  |  |  |  |  |  |  |  |
| 5 | 21 | 16 | 12 | 8 |  |  |  |  |  |  |  |  |  |  |  |
| 8 | 23 | 19 | 15 | 11 | 7 |  |  |  |  |  |  |  |  |  |  |
| 0 | 26 | 22 | 18 | 14 | 10 | 6 |  |  |  |  |  |  |  |  |  |
| 2 | 27 | 24 | 20 | 16 | 13 | 9 | 6 |  |  |  |  |  |  |  |  |
| 4 | 30 | 26 | 23 | 19 | 15 | 12 | 8 | 5 |  |  |  |  |  |  |  |
| 6 | 32 | 28 | 25 | 21 | 18 | 14 | 11 | 8 |  |  |  |  |  |  |  |
| 8 | 34 | 30 | 27 | 23 | 20 | 17 | 14 | 10 | 7 |  |  |  |  |  |  |
| 9 | 36 | 32 | 29 | 26 | 22 | 19 | 16 | 13 | 10 | 7 |  |  |  |  |  |
| 1 | 37 | 34 | 31 | 28 | 24 | 21 | 18 | 15 | 12 | 9 | 6 |  |  |  |  |
| 2 | 39 | 36 | 32 | 29 | 26 | 23 | 20 | 17 | 14 | 12 | 9 | 6 |  |  |  |
| 4 | 40 | 37 | 34 | 31 | 28 | 25 | 22 | 19 | 17 | 14 | 12 | 9 | 6 |  |  |
| 5 | 42 | 39 | 36 | 33 | 30 | 27 | 24 | 21 | 19 | 16 | 12 | 11 | 8 | 6 |  |
| 6 | 43 | 40 | 37 | 34 | 31 | 29 | 26 | 23 | 20 | 18 | 15 | 13 | 10 | 8 | 5 |
| 7 | 44 | 41 | 39 | 36 | 33 | 30 | 28 | 25 | 22 | 20 | 17 | 15 | 12 | 10 | 8 |
| 9 | 46 | 43 | 40 | 37 | 34 | 32 | 29 | 26 | 24 | 21 | 19 | 17 | 14 | 12 | 10 |
| 0 | 47 | 44 | 41 | 38 | 36 | 33 | 31 | 28 | 26 | 23 | 21 | 18 | 16 | 14 | 12 |
| 1 | 48 | 45 | 42 | 40 | 37 | 34 | 32 | 29 | 27 | 25 | 22 | 20 | 18 | 16 | 13 |
| 2 | 49 | 46 | 43 | 41 | 38 | 36 | 33 | 31 | 28 | 26 | 24 | 22 | 19 | 17 | 12 |
| 2 | 50 | 47 | 44 | 42 | 39 | 37 | 35 | 32 | 30 | 28 | 25 | 23 | 21 | 19 | 17 |
| 3 | 51 | 48 | 45 | 43 | 40 | 38 | 36 | 33 | 31 | 29 | 27 | 25 | 22 | 20 | 18 |
| 4 | 51 | 49 | 46 | 44 | 41 | 39 | 37 | 35 | 32 | 30 | 28 | 26 | 24 | 22 | 20 |
| 5 | 52 | 50 | 47 | 45 | 42 | 40 | 38 | 36 | 33 | 31 | 29 | 27 | 25 | 23 | 21 |
| 6 | 53 | 51 | 48 | 46 | 43 | 41 | 39 | 37 | 35 | 32 | 30 | 28 | 26 | 24 | 23 |
| 6 | 54 | 51 | 49 | 47 | 44 | 42 | 40 | 38 | 36 | 34 | 32 | 30 | 28 | 26 | 24 |

difference in wet- and dry-bulb readings. The number listed at that intersection is the relative humidity.

How do the humidity readings from the different sites compare? Is the amount of water released by the trees in a forest enough to affect the humidity?

# Profiles in the Earth:
# A Look at Soil Horizons

In a year's time, more than a ton of leaves, seeds, flowers, and branches rain down on an acre of forest floor. These materials gradually decompose as they are attacked by bacteria, fungi, and insects in the soil.

The result is a rich, dark, spongy mulch called **humus**. As any gardener knows, humus contributes essential nutrients to the soil and improves its texture. The countless meanderings of earthworms and other tunnelers mix humus into the soil.

To get a better look at what lies below the forest floor, you'll need a shovel, resealable plastic bags, a Bunsen burner (or outdoor gas grill), an oven, a permanent marker, a meterstick, a scale (lab, kitchen, or postal), a soil survey map, a metal tray, a crucible (or old metal container), tongs (or heavy-duty oven mitts), safety glasses, and your journal.

Contact your local soil conservation office to obtain a soil survey map of your area. You can find the telephone number in the blue pages of your telephone book. Look under the U.S. government listings for the Department of Agriculture, Natural Resources Conservation Service.

Use the soil survey map to find land areas with similar soils. Within these areas, try to locate a wooded area, a grassy field, and a bare dirt field, such as a construction site. When you go to each site, take a shovel, plastic bags, a permanent marker, a meterstick, and your journal. In an out-of-the-way place, dig a hole at least 1 meter (3.3 ft.) deep. Study the exposed soil along the sides of the hole. What do you see?

Because the processes of soil formation takes place from the surface down, you'll see layers, or **horizons**, of different color and composition. In a forest, the top layer consists mostly of decaying leaves. It is called the O horizon. This dark thin, layer feels soft when you rub it between your fingers. Below this layer is the A horizon, which consists of topsoil and is full of plant roots. The A horizon is a mixture of humus and fine particles from Earth's crust. When you rub the materials from this layer between your fingers, they feel a little gritty. The next layer, the B horizon, may be gray or streaked with red or yellow. The soil in this layer contains more clay than the layers above it. Below this is a rocky layer called the C horizon. It overlies bedrock, a layer of solid rock.

Measure the depth and width of each layer. Include a sketch in your journal. Note color and textures. Which horizon appears to have the most humus? You can test for humus back at your school lab or at home. To do this, collect a soil sample of each layer at each site. Store individual samples in resealable plastic bags. Record site information on the bags and in your journal. ***Fill up the hole when you are done.***

Back in the lab, spread a soil sample out in a metal tray. Remove any small stones. Dry the sample in a oven overnight at 100°C (212°F). Weigh out 30 to 60 grams (1 to 2 oz.) of dry soil. Add the soil to a crucible or small metal container. Place the crucible on a support stand over a Bunsen burner. ***Wear safety glasses when using the burner!*** Heat the soil until it is red hot. This will burn off the organic matter. Continue heating for 15 minutes.

After heating, let the container cool before moving it. Handle it with tongs or mitts. Reweigh the sample and then determine the fraction of organic matter using the formula given below.

$$\text{percent organic matter} = \frac{\text{initial weight of dried soil} - \text{final weight}}{\text{initial weight of dried soil}} \times 100$$

If more than 10 percent of your sample is organic matter, the soil is high in organic matter. If it is less than 2 percent organic matter, it is low in organic matter. Sort and heat your other soil samples.

If you're doing this experiment at home, ask permission before drying soil samples indoors. Some soils may stink up the house! Instead, you can use an outdoor gas grill set on high. Be sure to use an old metal tray when heating the soil. The high heat may warp the pan. Weigh at least 142 g (5 oz.) of dry soil. *Follow the same safety precautions you would use if you were using a Bunsen burner!*

### ✔ Doing More

Look for soil horizons already revealed in roadcuts or eroded stream banks. Scrape off the weathered surface with a shovel to get a better view. Compare soil horizons of a deciduous wooded area and a coniferous wooded area.

## Shielding the Ground

An oak tree has hundreds of thousands of leaves in its crown. Like tiny parasols, they shield the ground from the effects of sun and rain. How much protection do they give the soil?

With some basic tools and supplies you can find out how these tiny parasols affect soil temperatures. Why is soil temperature important? Most plants will only grow well in soils with temperatures between 16 and 22°C (61 and 72°F). To measure soil temperature you'll need a laboratory thermometer, a watch, a shovel, a ruler, a meterstick, graph paper, and your journal. Purchase a thermometer from one of the science suppliers listed at the back of this book or borrow one from your school science lab.

Try this activity in the summer. Find a wooded area, grassy field, and construction site or baseball field near your home. To compare soil temperatures in these three locations, take readings at the same time of day under similar weather conditions. Note the air temperature and weather conditions in your journal.

At each site, take temperature readings at every 10 centimeters (4 in.) of depth from the surface to a total depth of 1 meter (3.3 ft.). ***Do not attempt to force the thermometer into the ground!*** Instead, dig a small hole. Every 10 centimeters (4 in.), use your fingers to scratch out a thumb-size depression at the bottom of the hole. Gently embed the bulb end of the thermometer in the depression and press some loose dirt around it. Allow the thermometer 15 to 30 minutes to reach the soil temperature. Record the temperature in your journal. Continue digging to the next depth and repeat the procedure. When you are finished, fill in the hole and replace the leaf litter on top.

When you get home, collect your journal, graph paper, a pencil, and a ruler. For each set of data, plot temperature on the horizontal axis and soil depth on the vertical axis.

Compare the graphs. Assuming most plant roots are restricted to the top 30 to 60 centimeters (1 to 2 ft.) of soil, which of the three locations provides the range of temperatures best suited for plant growth?

# CHAPTER 3

# A First Look at the Forest: Describing and Measuring the Woods

WHAT DO YOU SEE WHEN YOU WALK into the woods? A bunch of trees and dead leaves? People who study and work in the forest see much more than this. A forester sizes up the trees and estimates how much wood can be cut from them. An **ecologist** notices the number of tree species and wonders which ones contribute the most to the forest community. A wildlife biologist looks along forest edges and scans the woods from top to bottom, seeing the forest in layers. These forest edges and layers are important habitats for many animals.

Although a forester, an ecologist, and a wildlife biologist view a forest in different ways, they all know how to define a forest. Do you? Most of us think we do. But is a stand of trees in a city park a forest? Is a Christmas tree farm a forest?

No! A forest is a complex and diverse community of plants and animals. The largest and most conspicuous members are the trees. Forest trees look different from other types of trees. Trees in a forest grow so close together that light is filtered from the lower branches, causing them to wither and die. Unlike city trees, which have lower branches within reach, a forest tree's lowest branches could be 12 meters (40 ft.) or more above the ground.

Even the ground looks different in a forest. A blanket of dead leaves, crisscrossed with rotting logs, covers the forest floor. These features are common to all forests, yet

*The crowns of a forest's trees form an effective light screen. Only where a gap occurs in the canopy, does bright sunlight stream in.*

forests across North America differ in many ways. How can we describe a particular forest?

One way to describe a forest is to measure the trees. A standard measurement uses the part of a tree that is easiest to reach—the trunk. The thickness, or diameter, of a tree trunk is usually taken at 1.5 meters (4.5 ft.) above the ground. This value is reported as the diameter at breast height (DBH). The heights of the tallest trees and other forest layers are also important measures of a forest.

No one can describe a forest without identifying its tree species. Before scientists describe a forest, they compile a list of the tree species to determine an area's **species diversity**. But that's not enough. Often a forest community is named after just one or two tree species. For example, across Michigan and Ohio, a beech-maple forest covers the land. Farther south spreads an oak-hickory forest. Many other tree species inhabit these woods, yet only these stand out. A tree species can dominate a woods by its relative abundance. But it can also overshadow the other trees by sheer size.

Of course, other species of plants and animals live in the woods. An examination of the forest, layer by layer, can reveal these forest inhabitants. The surface of the canopy is a world of intense heat, violent winds, and pelting rain. Few animals can withstand such conditions. Yet just below, life is abundant. Here insects feed on the leaves, sucking the juices through spear-shaped beaks, munching on whole leaves, or dining on the soft tissues within. Birds such as vireos, warblers, and flycatchers dart between the branches, nabbing unwary insects. Squirrels are also at home in the canopy. Sometimes even porcupines may be seen on a high branch eating young leaves and twigs.

Look for the flying squirrel and many songbirds in the understory. You may even see a bird nest in the fork of an understory tree. The canopy above protects animals in the understory from storms and flying predators. Yet animals in the understory are also far enough above the ground to avoid hunters that roam the forest floor.

*Eastern chipmunks gather acorns from the forest floor and store them in underground burrows. They also eat berries, seeds, and insects.*

Shrubs, which often form a tangle of woody growth, provide shelter and food for some birds, insects, and small mammals. Shrub berries and seeds are favorite foods for many of these creatures. Small, burrowing mammals such as deer mice, chipmunks, and shrews often seek cover in the shrub layer as they forage for food on the forest floor.

Ferns, lichens, and wildflowers form the lowest layers of the forest. The pollen and nectar of the flowers attracts insects throughout spring and summer. Other insects feed on the green leaves. Insects, snakes, mice, turtles, and some birds wander between the leafy stalks, where they are well hidden.

Countless insects and spiders crawl between the fallen leaves while earthworms till the soil. Soil bacteria and fungi work at decomposing the fallen litter.

From top to bottom, a forest is home to a variety of plants and animals. But nowhere is this variety greater than along the forest's edges. Where a forest merges with an open field or makes way for a river or stream, two differing habitats converge. Here you will find greater numbers and a greater variety of wildlife than in either of the habitats. Scientists refer to this phenomenon as the edge effect.

Use the activities that follow to take an in-depth look at a nearby woods. Step off the beaten path. But before you do, review the rules for safety and good sense in the Introduction. Do you know how to use a compass to find your way? Look over this chapter's first activity to refresh your memory or learn this basic skill for the first time.

PROJECT **4**

## Steering a Course through the Woods: How to Use a Compass

Exploring the woods can be an exciting adventure. If you stick to well-marked trails and pay attention to where you're going, you may never have a problem finding your way.

But suppose you want to step off the trail? Perhaps you've spotted an unusual tree across a ravine, but you don't have a map. Once you've left the trail, will you know how to get back?

For this type of exploration, you'll need a compass, a watch, surveyor's flagging or strips of fabric, and your journal. Hiking and camping supply stores offer a wide variety of compasses. For basic field use, look for a compass with a clear plastic base plate and a fluid-filled rotating capsule. Some compasses have a sighting mirror that allows you to view an object ahead and read the compass at the same time.

Once you've selected a compass, take a minute to study its parts. The most important part is the magnetic needle inside the compass housing. See Figure 8. This needle aligns itself with Earth's magnetic field and always points north.* Beneath the needle, etched in the compass housing, is the north-south arrow. The outer edge of the compass housing

---

*The compass needle points to magnetic north, not true north. From any point on Earth, true north may lie several degrees from magnetic north. The difference between magnetic north and true north is called declination.

**Figure 8**  The Parts of a Compass

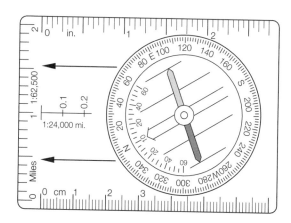

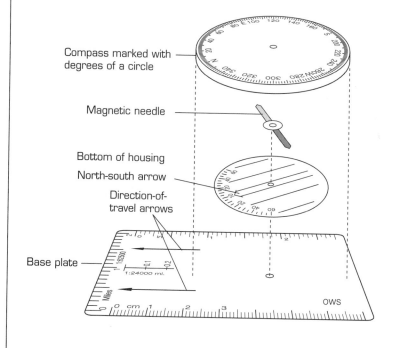

Compass marked with degrees of a circle

Magnetic needle

Bottom of housing
North-south arrow

Direction-of-travel arrows

Base plate

is marked off in numbers up to 360. These numbers represent the degrees of a circle. The compass housing sits on a clear base plate. Note the direction-of-travel arrow on the base plate.

To use your compass, hold it level in the palms of your hands. Your hands should be positioned away from your body at waist height. Keep your elbows pressed against your sides and the compass away from metal objects. Stand still as the compass needle swings back and forth before coming to rest. Orient the compass by twisting the housing to align the needle with the north-south arrow. You can now read the direction to any object by sighting off the compass housing.

To travel in a specific direction or toward a distant landmark and back requires following a compass bearing. To take a bearing, point the direction-of-travel arrow at a landmark. Twist the compass housing to line up the compass needle with the north-south arrow. Read the bearing on the outer edge of the compass housing, where it touches the direction-of-travel arrow on the base plate.

Remember that number, or better yet, write it down! Now walk toward the landmark following the compass bearing. To hold a true course, make sure you are holding the compass steady and that the compass needle is lined up exactly with the north-south arrow.

To find your way back, calculate the bearing you'll need to travel to retrace your steps. The new bearing will be 180° from your original bearing. If you began by walking a course bearing of 160°, you'll return by a bearing of 340°. Readjust the compass housing so that your new bearing is aligned with the direction-of-travel arrow. Holding the compass steady in your palms, turn your body slowly until the compass needle is directly in line with the north-south arrow. Follow the direction-of-travel arrow for your return trip.

Now that you know how to use a compass, you probably feel like you're all set to blaze new trails through the woods. But not so fast! Practice using your compass in your backyard or neighborhood before you enter the woods.

When you do go into the woods, take along a few friends. Tell a responsible adult where you're going and when you plan to return. In the beginning, use surveyor's flagging or strips of fabric to mark your way. When you leave a trail, walk only 5 minutes into the woods. Use your compass skills to direct you back to the trail.

### ✔ Doing More

To navigate safely in the woods, it is best to use a compass and a map. The map most commonly used by hikers is called a **topographic map.** Contact the United States Geologic Survey to obtain a free booklet on using these maps. See the For Further Information section at the back of this book for the agency's address.

Practice using a map and compass together to find your way. Join an orienteering club. Orienteering is a timed cross-country sport that involves using a map and compass to navigate through a course marked only by designated control points that each player must visit.

PROJECT **5**

# Sizing Up the Trees

How do you measure a forest? The easiest way is to size up the trees. Common tree measurements include height and trunk diameter. Foresters collect this information to estimate the amount of wood that can be cut from the standing trees. Even if you're not interested in lumber, you'll need to know these measurements before you can describe a forest.

To measure trees, you'll need the following tools and supplies: a compass, diameter tape or tailor's measuring tape, a calculator, a clinometer, a 7.5-meter (25-ft.) measuring tape, and your journal. Directions for making your own diameter tape and clinometer are included in the Appendix at the back of this book. The For Further Information section lists suppliers that sell these items.

Throw everything into a backpack and head to your favorite wooded area. *Wear long pants and socks to protect your legs from poison ivy. Do you know what this plant looks like? Make sure you do before you enter the woods!*

Hike along a marked trail until you locate a large tree you'd like to measure. With a tape measure, locate the point on the trunk that's 1.5 meters (4.5 ft.) above the ground. If the tree sits on a slope, measure from the uphill side of the trunk. Run a diameter tape around the trunk at that point. Read the diameter directly off the specially marked scale on the tape.

If you are using a tailor's tape, measure the distance around the trunk, or the circumference, 1.5 meters (4.5 ft.) off the ground. Calculate the trunk's diameter using the following formula.

$$\text{diameter} = \frac{\text{circumference}}{3.14}$$

Next measure the height of the tree. You can use a clinometer. Measure to the top of the crown, and record the information in your journal.

In the same forest, search for larger trees. What are the measurements of the largest tree you can find?

### ✔ Doing More

Is there a giant among the forest trees in your woods? Perhaps it's big enough to be included in the National Register of Big Trees. Write American Forests for information on nominating a champion tree. The address is listed in the For Further Information section at the back of this book.

# From Top to Bottom:
# The Vertical Structure of a Forest

A forest may be arranged in many layers or in just a few, but all forests are multistoried communities. Try describing the plants and animals of a local wooded area in terms of these forest layers: canopy, understory, shrub layer, herb layer, and ground layer. (See the Introduction to review these terms).

To measure the height of each layer, you'll need a 6-meter (20-ft.) extendible pole marked in 1-meter (3.3-ft.) increments, a measuring tape with a minimum length of 7.5 meters (25 ft.), graph paper, a ruler, a clinometer, and your journal. You'll also need the help of at least one friend. You can make your own extendible pole and a clinometer using the instructions in the Appendix at the back of this book.

Visit a nearby forest in the spring or early summer. This is the best time to observe the herb layer. ***Beware of poison ivy! Wear thick socks and long pants to protect your legs.*** Starting with the lowest forest layers, measure the heights of some plants. Use the extendible pole to measure all layers beneath the canopy. To measure the canopy, use a clinometer, a friend, and a measuring tape. To measure tree height, follow the directions given in the Appendix at the back of this book. Record the heights in your journal. Take at least ten measurements for each layer. Record descriptions of the plants, too. Note the category of trees that makes up the canopy layer—are they conifers, deciduous trees, or both?

Calculate the average height for each forest layer by adding all measurements for a single layer and dividing by the number of readings. Use a bar graph to present your results. Let the vertical axis represent average height, and the horizontal axis represent the forest layer.

How many layers are present in the woods you explored? How tall is the canopy layer? Study both a coniferous and a deciduous forest. How many layers are present in each?

While the forest is home to many creatures, most restrict their activities to just one or two forest layers. There they forage for food, find mates, rest, and carry out their daily lives. Each forest layer provides unique habitats for wildlife. In general, forests with fewer layers support smaller populations and fewer varieties of animal life than forests with many layers.

As you explore the woods, look for animal life in each layer. Record your observations in your journal. Some scientists consider the trunks of the canopy trees to be an additional forest layer. What creatures can you find living there?

PROJECT **7**

## Looking at a Representative Plot

How many species of trees are present in your favorite woods? Which are common? Which are rare? One way to find out is to survey representative plots.

To do this type of inventory, you'll need a tree identification guide, a 7.5-meter (25-ft.) measuring tape, tent stakes, surveyor's flagging or strips of brightly colored fabric, a compass, a chalk bag, your journal, and several friends. You can make a chalk bag using instructions found in the Appendix at the back of this book.

Pick a wooded area near your home to survey. If you are more familiar with species of conifers, choose a coniferous woods. If you're able to identify deciduous trees more readily, be sure to select this type of forest.

Once you're in the woods, step off the trail and mark an area that measures $7 \times 14$ meters, or approximately 100 m² ($23 \times 46$ ft.). Use surveyor's flagging or strips of fabric to establish the corners and sides of the rectangle. Tie flagging to tree limbs, shrubs, or stakes placed in the ground. Make a rough sketch in your journal of the location of this plot. Take compass readings to include on your map. Assign the plot a number in your journal.

Once the plot is marked, identify each tree species and count the number of individuals of each species. Limit your census taking to mature trees—trees with a minimum DBH of 8 centimeters (3 in.) or a circumference of 25 centimeters (10 in.). When you've identified a tree and recorded the information in your journal, mark the trunk with the chalk bag by giving it a friendly whap.

Randomly select a few more areas of the woods, and survey them. In each case, mark the boundaries, identify the mature trees, and count the number of individual trees of each species. Record all your findings in your journal.

How many tree species characterize the woods you explored? Which trees are most abundant? Forests vary in their diversity. Some forests, like the cove hardwood forest of the Great Smoky Mountains, are very diverse. An acre of these woods might contain thirty to forty species of trees. The boreal forest is much less diverse, with fewer than ten species per acre.

### ✔ Doing More

How do you know when you've surveyed enough plots to draw reliable conclusions? Here's a way to find out. After surveying five plots, copy Table 3 in your journal and fill it in to summarize all your data.

The cumulative area sampled refers to the total area of all plots surveyed. To compute the cumulative number of new species, start with the number of species from your first plot. Add to that the numbers of new species identified in each additional plot. You can use the information in the table to graph the cumulative number of species (vertical axis) versus the cumulative area sampled (horizontal axis). What conclusions can you draw from your graph?

| Table 3 | Surveying a Wooded Area | | | |
|---|---|---|---|---|
| Plot Number | Cumulative Area Sampled $(m^2)$ | Number of Tree Species | Number of New Species | Cumulative Number of New Species |
| 1 | 100 | | | |
| 2 | 200 | | | |
| 3 | 300 | | | |
| 4 | 400 | | | |
| 5 | 500 | | | |

If the curve on your graph rises sharply and then levels off, you probably have enough data to draw reliable conclusions. If your curve does not level off, you need to survey a few more plots. Add the new data to your species-area curve and reevaluate.

# Spotting Woodland Birds

Have you ever hiked through a forest and wondered where all the animals are? The trick to finding them is knowing when, where, and how to look. Of all forest wildlife, birds are often the easiest to spot.

You don't need any equipment to watch birds, but a pair of binoculars and a field guide will make the experience more enjoyable. Binoculars can give you a better view of a bird hidden in the brush or perched high on a branch. Try borrowing a pair—from a friend, neighbor, or your school's science department. A few good field guides are listed in the For Further Information section at the back of this book.

Most forests in North America have two sets of bird populations: the permanent residents and the migrants. The permanent residents are present year-round, while the migrants appear in the spring to select mates, breed, and raise their young. In the fall, they return to their winter homes. On any given day, birds are most active early in the morning and from late afternoon to sunset. You'll see the fewest birds during the hottest part of the day—midafternoon. To see the most birds, try to be in the woods on a spring day just as the sun is rising.

Now that you're in the right place at the right time, here are a few more hints to start you on your birding adventure:

- Because loud noises cause most wildlife to seek cover, walk quietly in the woods.

*Forest birds, such as this Kentucky warbler, are most active in the early morning and late afternoon.*

- Keep talk to a minimum.
- Stop often. Stand still, look around you, and listen.
- Scan the canopy, the understory, the shrubs, and along forest edges for a glimpse of birds.
- Keep an eye out for the darting movement of a bird as it goes from one perch to another. Use your binoculars to follow the bird to its new perch.

  Look for birds searching for insects on the trunks of forest trees. Some birds, like woodpeckers, are easy to spot. Others, such as brown creepers or nuthatches, are harder to see.

You can locate some birds by listening carefully. A drumming or tapping sound in the woods alerts you that a woodpecker is nearby. Many birds give short calls to warn against predators and longer songs to attract mates or protect a territory against an invader. Some birds, like the ground-dwelling grouse, make a variety of noises as they beat and clap their wings during courtship displays.

Although silence is the general rule when viewing wildlife, you can actually attract some birds by calling to them. Songbirds may hop out to the end of a branch if you call "*pissh, pissh, pissh, pissh.*"

### ✔ Doing More

Learn to identify the birds you see. A good field guide will explain the features and behaviors that help birders identify birds. Find out if there is a birding club in your community—your local library may have this information.

The National Audubon Society is an organization dedicated to the conservation of birds and other wildlife. They have local chapters across the country that sponsor monthly birding events. Find out if there's a chapter in your area, and attend one of their meetings or outings. You can contact this organization using information listed in the For Further Information section at the back of this book.

PROJECT **9**

## Take a Walk on the Wild Side: The Search for Woodland Mammals

In your walks in the woods, how many mammals have you come across? Besides deer or squirrels, probably not too many! Many mammals are active only at night. Some are easily frightened by the sounds humans make and quickly seek a hiding place. You can catch a glimpse of some of these creatures or find clues to their whereabouts if you know when, where, and how to look.

You won't need much equipment beyond a tape measure, your journal, and a pencil or pen. You may also wish to take along a field guide to mammals or animal tracks. (Some field guides are listed in the For Further Information section at the back of this book.) If you head to the woods before dawn or at dusk, pack a flashlight.

Dawn and dusk are the best times to see animals. Both day-active and nocturnal animals may be about. Of course, you'll never see them if you travel down the trail at breakneck speed. Slow down and stop often. Walk quietly and keep your voice low if you're hiking with others.

Where should you look for mammals? While you might find them anywhere in the forest, you'll improve your chances if you head to a woodland stream or pond, or a spot where the forest borders a field. Find a secluded spot and sit down. If the wind is blowing, sit downwind so the animals won't detect your scent.

Plan to be settled in before the sun rises or as the sun sets. Watch for movements. Look for parts of an animal, like the tail of a white-tailed deer—sometimes you won't see the whole animal. Listen for the sounds of animals as well. Record your observations in your journal.

You can also look for traces and tracks. Mammals sometime leave evidence of their activities and movements in the woods. Footprints or tracks left in snow, soft mud, or wet sand are obvious clues. But other signs include scat (droppings), nests, dens, burrows, fur caught on a bush or barbed wire, scratchings and rubbings made on bark by claws or antlers, teeth marks on bark or twigs, and piles of half-eaten seeds or cones spread out on a tree stump.

Tracks are often the best clues to an animal's identity. If you find a set or even just one footprint, count the number of toes and claws. Measure the width and length of each print without the claws. Make a rough sketch in your journal. A field guide to mammals will help you identify the animal that made the tracks.

Other signs may be harder to spot. Try looking for droppings on one visit and nests and burrows or markings on bark or twigs on the next. Study a field guide before you go. Always take your journal to record what you find.

Pay attention to the small things. For example, when you find damage to bark or twigs, note the type of damage. Deer and elk rub their antlers against tree trunks, leaving the bark

*What's happened here? What clues can you find that might tell you a bear was here? (Hint: Look at the height of the marks above the ground and the width of each set of claw marks.)*

in shreds. Bears often claw and bite the bark, pulling it completely off the trunk. You may see it lying at the base of the tree. Long vertical slash marks might have been left by a mountain lion that was sharpening its claws. If you see teethmarks on a branch, measure the width of the marks. If a twig has been gnawed, note if the cut is ragged or blunt. From small clues like these, you can learn a lot about the animals that live in the woods.

# CHAPTER 4

# Oh, What a Tangled Web: The Ways of Life in the Forest

LIKE THE FOLKS IN A SMALL MOUNtain community of a century ago where everyone seemed to be kin, the members of a forest community are intricately bound to each other. But the relationships in a forest weren't created in a day or even a few years. They have evolved over millions of years.

Competition is a common thread in the web of forest life, even among plants. Forest plants compete for light, moisture, and nutrients. The roots and crowns of trees jostle for greater growing space. In this slow but steady struggle, some win and flourish, while others lose and eventually die. The battle may involve chemical warfare. Chemicals released by roots or leached from leaves inhibit seed ger-

*The lichens growing on the bark of this hickory are not harming the tree.*

mination or growth in neighboring plants. This phenomenon is called **al-lelopathy.**

But not all associations in the forest are so unfriendly. In some cases, one party benefits while the other is unaffected. This type of association is called **commensalism.** For example, one commensal partner often gets a free ride on the back of another. In the woods of North America, mosses and lichens grow on tree trunks. In tropical forests, orchids, ferns, and bromeliads drape from every branch.

In other cases, both parties benefit. This type of association is called **mutualism.** In some pine forests, tree roots meet and fuse. This allows the exchange of sugars and other nutrients. A mutualistic relationship that involves individuals of different species is called **symbiosis.** In coniferous woods, fungi may form close associations with tree roots. The conifers depend on the fungi to pull essential nutrients from the soil. The fungi benefit from the sugars produced by the trees. Neither would be able to grow alone in the nutrient-poor, dry, sandy soils where conifers are commonly found.

Complex relationships exist between plants and animals, too. Many plants rely on animals to help them spread their seeds to other sites. Dry fruits often have barbs or small hooks that catch on animals' fur. Some soft fruits are eaten by birds and mammals, which then eliminate the waste products far away from the parent plant. When acorns and other nuts are buried by squirrels—and then forgotten—they may sprout.

The activities in this chapter will help you learn more about the fascinating relationships in a forest.

## Chemical Warfare among the Plants

Some plants pack a chemical arsenal in their leaves and roots. A silent battle with neighboring plants begins as the chemicals leak out into the surrounding soil.

Which woodland plants in your area engage in these silent battles? To find out, you'll need a package of radish seeds, a kitchen or postal scale, a ruler, white paper towels, plastic sandwich bags, a graduated cylinder or measuring cup, a pipette or tablespoon, distilled water, a stovetop or microwave oven, cheesecloth, a funnel, a container for boiling water, several jars with lids, and your journal. A field guide to trees and shrubs and a field guide to wildflowers and weeds would also be helpful.

Select a few trees, shrubs, or nonwoody plants to test for the production of harmful chemicals. Look especially for a black walnut or a tree of heaven. Both are known to produce inhibitory substances. Collect twenty leaves from each plant you wish to test. Keep the leaves from the same plant together, stored in a plastic sandwich bag. Label and date each bag. Refrigerate the samples as soon as you return from the woods.

The first step in processing your samples is to leach the chemicals out of the leaves with boiling water. The watery soup that's produced is called an extract. To make an extract, weigh out 28 grams (1 oz.) of leaves from one plant. Tear the leaves into small pieces. Boil 200 milliliters (1 cup) of water on the stove or in the microwave. Remove the boiling water from the heat source. ***Be careful! Both the water and steam rising from the surface could burn you!***

Immediately place the shredded leaves into the boiling water. Let the mixture cool. While it's cooling, set a funnel inside the opening of a small jar. Line the inside of the funnel with cheesecloth. Pour the cooled water and leafy material into the funnel. Discard the shredded leaves and label the jar containing the extract. Put the lid on the jar and store the extract in the refrigerator while you finish making extracts of other leaf samples.

Radish seeds germinate in 5 to 7 days and are sensitive to inhibitory chemicals. Before you test your extracts on germinating radish seeds, do a test run. This will allow you to observe how the seeds grow and develop normally. Fold a paper towel to fit inside a plastic sandwich bag. Add enough distilled water to just wet the towel, without leaving any excess water. Place ten radish seeds on top of the towel and close the bag. **Incubate** the seeds by storing the bag at room temperature in a dark place.

Check the bags after 4 days. Measure the shoots or roots of several plants. If most are at least 20 millimeters ($\frac{3}{4}$ in.) long, use this incubation period for the rest of the experiment. If the seedlings are shorter than 20 millimeters ($\frac{3}{4}$ in.), return them to the bag and incubate them for an additional day or two.

Once you know how long it takes for radish seedlings to grow, test each extract. Using a separate plastic bag for each extract sample, add a few milliliters (or tablespoons) of extract to a folded paper towel. Place the paper towel inside the appropriate bag and add ten radish seedlings. Label each bag and incubate all the bags. At the same time, run a control that consists of a sandwich bag with ten seedlings, a paper towel, and water—but no extract. After the incubation period, examine the seedlings in each bag. Measure the length of each shoot and root. Record the data in your journal.

To analyze your data, determine the average shoot and root growth for the seedlings in each plastic bag. Add the lengths of all the shoots and divide that value by the number of seedlings measured. Do the same for root lengths. Which extracts appeared to inhibit radish germination?

### ✔ Doing More

Among seeds receiving the same extract, did you notice variation in shoot or root lengths? Variation is normal and expected, due to differences in the genetic makeup of each seed. But how much variation is normal? And how can we compare the control group and treatment groups with so much variation in each?

Ask your math teacher to help you use some basic statistics to analyze your results. For example, try using the Student's t test to compare controls to treatment groups.

PROJECT **10**

# Bear Hunting with a Microscope

A little-known creature ambles slowly on wide, stumpy legs. Four pairs of legs paw their way through a thin film of water. The animal, a tardigrade, is less than 1 millimeter (0.04 in.) in length. Because it has a round body, stubby legs, and lumbers along, it is commonly known as the water bear.

The water bear lives in droplets of water on mosses and lichens. This little creature has an unusual ability—it can survive without water for long periods of time. When the water it lives in dries up, the animal goes into a special desiccated state called a tun.

Look for tardigrades in a wooded area near your home. You'll need a pocket knife, a hand trowel, and plastic sandwich

*A tardigrade's claws help it cling to the surface of moss and lichens.*

bags to collect materials that may contain tardigrades. When you return to your home or to school, you'll need petri dishes or small custard or pudding cups, distilled or spring water, a medicine dropper or pipette, forceps, and a dissecting microscope to examine these minute animals. You can borrow a dissecting microscope from your school's science lab.

Find an area where lichens and mosses are abundant. Lichens are leafy or crusty organisms that can be found on tree trunks and large rocks. Many lichens are pale green. Use your pocket knife to remove lichens or a hand trowel to collect mosses. You may have to remove some bark with the lichen sample. Place each sample in a separate plastic sandwich bag. Label and date the bag. Include information in your journal about the collection site.

When you return home or to school, set up several custard cups or petri dishes. If you're using custard cups, add 1 to 2 centimeters ($\frac{1}{2}$ to 1 in.) of distilled or spring water. Fill the petri dishes half full. Soak each lichen or moss upside down in the container. The tardigrades will fall to the bottom of the dish. If the water bears are in an inactive state, it will take 1 and 3 days to activate them.

On the third day, remove the lichen or moss sample from each dish. Shake any excess water into the dish, then store the sample in its original sandwich bag.

Examine the water in each dish using a dissecting microscope. Water bears can be up to 1.2 millimeters (0.05 in.) long but most are about half that size. Look for them crawling about on clumps of debris.

Can you identify different kinds of tardigrades? In your journal, try sketching the water bears you observe.

#### ✔ Doing More

Take a closer look at the lichens that harbor tardigrades. (Check the For Further Information section at the back of this book for an appropriate field guide.) These organisms are made up of algae and fungus that live together. Use a single-edged razor blade to cut a thin section of lichen. A hand lens or microscope will help you identify the algal cells and the long, thin **hyphae** of the fungus.

# A Gut-Level Attraction: Protozoans and Their Termite Hosts

Luckily for trees and other woody plants, only a few animals can digest wood. The termite is one of the few that can. With its strong mouthparts, termites bite and chew wood into small pieces. **Protozoans** and other microscopic organisms inside the termite's gut finish digesting the wood. A termite and the creatures in its digestive system have a symbiotic relationship. Each organism helps the other.

To observe this unusual partnership, you will need a compound microscope, microscope slides, coverslips, forceps, a scalpel or single-edged razor blade, a teaspoon, a measuring cup, salt, water, a garbage bag, a shovel, and small collecting jars.

To collect termites, plan a trip to a local wooded area in late spring or summer. Choose an area with plenty of fallen logs or branches. Search for wood that shows signs of decay—lots of holes and tunnels; soft, moist, spongy wood; and decomposed organic material or humus that looks like soil.

With quick, sharp blows of a shovel, chop off a piece of a rotting log. You may see small, white, antlike creatures scurrying about. These are termites. They have a somewhat flattened abdomen, but lack the thin waist that is characteristic of ants. Termites are sensitive to light and will try to hurry back into their tunnels, so you'll need to move quickly to catch them. Use forceps to place them in a collecting jar with small fragments of the log. Transport larger pieces of the log in a garbage bag.

Back at home, make a dilute salt (saline) solution to observe the other member of this symbiotic duo. Add $\frac{1}{2}$ teaspoon of salt to 1 cup of water. Stir to dissolve. Place a drop of saline on a clean microscope slide. Using forceps and a scalpel or razor blade, remove the abdomen of one termite.

Transfer the abdomen to the slide containing a drop of saline. With forceps, squeeze the abdomen so that the intestines spill out onto the slide. Tear apart the intestines to release the protozoans into the saline solution. Remove the larger pieces of tissue, and add a coverslip. View under the high power objective of a compound microscope. Look for teardrop-shaped, single-celled organisms with thin, whiplike hairs. The hairs are not really hairs at all. They are special organs called **flagella.**

When you have completed your observations, return any large pieces of the log and any living termites to the woods. ***Termites can be highly destructive! Doublecheck your work area before you leave. Do not leave any living termites in your house or school!***

## Habitats for the Homeless:
## Building Nest Boxes for the Birds

During its lifetime, a tree provides food and shelter for an amazing number of creatures. But this doesn't end with the death of the tree. Even after its death, the tree serves as shelter and a source of food for some organisms.

Dead standing trees are called **snags**. Many birds and small mammals build their nests in holes and cavities they create or find in snags. Some people consider these dead trees a safety hazard and remove them from the woods. When snags are cut down and taken away, forest creatures lose their homes.

You can provide these displaced snag-dwellers with alternative housing. To construct homes for the downy woodpecker—a year-round resident in most parts of the United States—you'll need binoculars, a field guide to birds, an extension ladder, a sharp butcher knife, coated wire or cording, brown latex spray paint, exterior grade construction adhesive (Liquid Nails is one trade name), and sheets or blocks of polystyrene foam board. Most home building suppliers will stock this as a type of insulation material.

The downy woodpecker is a woodland bird that's also commonly seen in suburbs and orchards. If you have a bird feeder in your backyard, you might even see this woodpecker coming in for a snack. Look for it in a nearby woods in the early morning or early evening.

Check your field guide's range map to make sure you live within the bird's normal range. If it doesn't live in your area, skip ahead to the Doing More section. If this bird lives in your area, but you're having trouble sighting it, contact a local chapter of the National Audubon Society for help. This organization's address is listed in the For Further Information section at the back of this book.

The downy woodpecker is a primary cavity nester—it nests only in a hole that it makes itself. Studies have shown,

*How can you tell this bird is a downy woodpecker? Look at its field marks.*

however, that this bird will use polystyrene blocks in place of a dead tree. Because most birds breed in the spring, fall or winter is a good time to start this project.

With a very sharp kitchen knife, carefully cut a block of polystyrene that measures 15 × 15 × 50 centimeters (6 × 6 × 20 in.). If you are working with polystyrene sheets, use adhesive to bond several sheets together to create a block with these dimensions. Spray the block with brown latex paint, and allow it to dry.

The block is now ready to be mounted in a tree or on a pole. You can put it up in your backyard or in a wooded area near your home. In either case, the block must be mounted 2 to 6 meters (6 to 20 ft.) off the ground. *If you need to use an extension ladder, ask an adult for help!* Position the polystyrene block vertically. Lash the top and bottom of the block to the tree or pole using rope or coated wire. See Figure 9 on the next page.

If possible, monitor the block daily. Note the appearance of any woodpecker holes and the date of cavity excavation. Observe the breeding pair as they incubate the eggs and raise their young. Try to keep a count of the number of young birds raised successfully. Check the nest after the woodpeckers have left to see if new occupants move in.

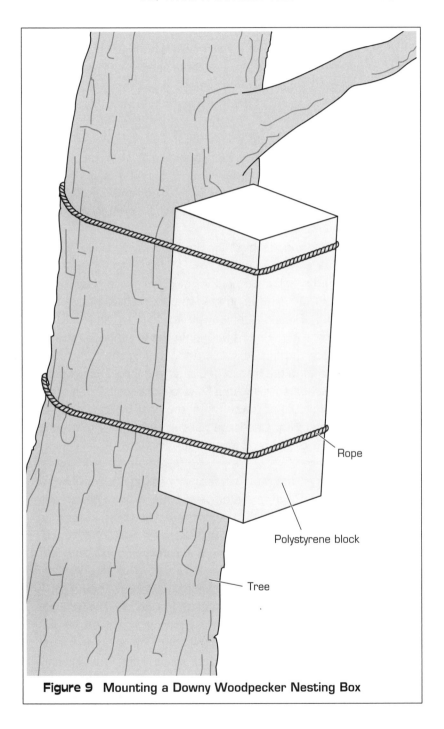

**Figure 9** Mounting a Downy Woodpecker Nesting Box

### ✔ Doing More

If woodpeckers don't live in your area, you could try building a wooden nesting box for a white-breasted nuthatch or a great crested flycatcher. But before you begin, make sure the bird you've selected has been sighted in your area.

- To build a white-breasted nuthatch nesting box, you'll need a $\frac{3}{4} \times 19 \times 16$ in. piece of white pine, $1\frac{1}{2}$-in. galvanized box nails, exterior grade wood glue, two 1-in. hinges, a saw, a hammer, and a drill with $\frac{1}{2}$-in. and $1\frac{1}{4}$-in. drill bits. *If you use an electric saw, work carefully and ask an adult to assist you.*

  Cut the wood pieces for the floor, back, sides, front, and roof, as shown in Figure 10. Using the $1\frac{1}{4}$-in. drill bit, drill the entrance hole in the front piece. Using the $\frac{1}{2}$-in. drill bit, drill five holes in the floor, so rainwater can drain out. Glue and nail the back, sides, and bottom pieces together. Before nailing on the front piece, attach the hinges to the back wall. After adding the front wall, nail the roof to the hinges. Make sure the roof hangs over the front wall so rainwater flows off the roof. The hinges will allow you to open the top of the nest box and clean it out each spring. Use large nails or heavy wire to mount the box 5 to 20 feet above the ground in a deciduous wooded area.

- To build a great crested flycatcher nesting box, you'll need a $\frac{3}{4} \times 21 \times 22$ in. piece of white pine, $1\frac{1}{2}$-in. galvanized box nails, exterior grade wood glue, two 1-in. hinges, a saw, a hammer, a drill with $\frac{1}{2}$-in. and 2-in. drill bits. *If you use an electric saw, work carefully and ask an adult to assist you.*

  Cut the wood for the floor, back, sides, front, and roof, as shown in Figure 11 on page 82. Use the 2-in. drill bit to drill an entrance hole in the front piece. Use the $\frac{1}{2}$-in. drill bit to make five holes in the floor. These holes will let rainwater drain out, so the nest will stay dry. Glue and nail the back, sides, and bottom pieces together. Before nailing on the front piece, attach the hinges to the back wall.

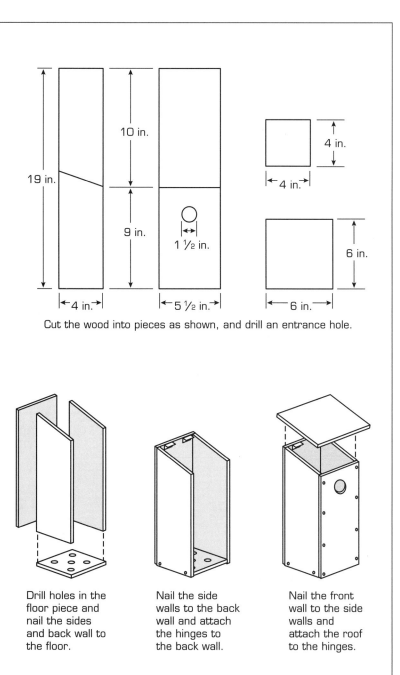

Cut the wood into pieces as shown, and drill an entrance hole.

Drill holes in the floor piece and nail the sides and back wall to the floor.

Nail the side walls to the back wall and attach the hinges to the back wall.

Nail the front wall to the side walls and attach the roof to the hinges.

**Figure 10** **Building a White-breasted Nuthatch Nesting Box**

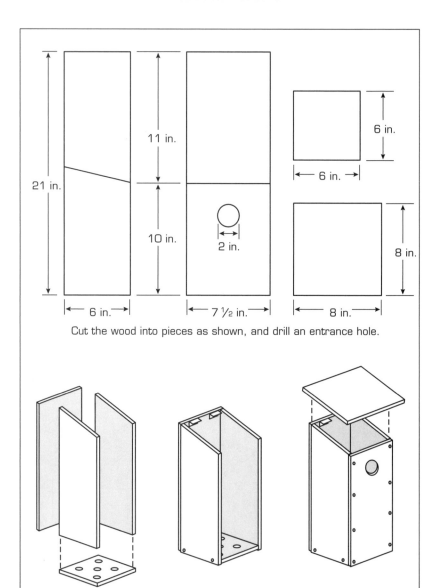

Cut the wood into pieces as shown, and drill an entrance hole.

Drill holes in the floor piece and nail the sides and back wall to the floor.

Nail the side walls to the back wall and attach the hinges to the back wall.

Nail the front wall to the side walls and attach the roof to the hinges.

**Figure 11**   **Building a Flycatcher Nesting Box**

After adding the front wall, nail the roof to the hinges. The roof should hang over the front wall, so rainwater will flows off the roof. You can use the hinges to open the nest box and clean it out each spring. Use large nails or heavy wire to mount the box 8 to 20 feet above the ground along the edge of a forest.

# The Forgetful Nature of Squirrels: How Squirrels Plant the Forest

Every fall, squirrels gather seeds. They eat as many as they can and store the rest. If you are in a forest, a park, or a yard, you can watch them scurrying across the ground, leaping through the trees, and burying acorns or nuts in the ground.

When winter comes and food is scarce, a squirrel may retrieve the nuts it has buried. The squirrel uses its sense of smell to find buried nuts, but it usually doesn't recover them all. If conditions are right, those nuts will germinate and grow into a tree.

How far do squirrels carry seeds? To answer this question, you will need a tape measure (minimum length of 7.5 meters [25 ft.]), binoculars, stakes and flagging or popsicle sticks, plenty of acorns, and your journal.

Begin by scouting out an area where squirrels are active. In late summer or fall, find some oak trees and gather a large sack of acorns. At sunrise, collect your equipment and a small sack of acorns, and go to your squirrel site. Spread the acorns at the base of an oak tree, find a secluded spot, and wait for squirrels to arrive. Plan to stay at the site for 1 to 2 hours.

Use binoculars to watch the squirrels eat and bury acorns. When a squirrel leaves, mark the spot where it buried acorns with popsicle sticks (in a park or your neigh-

*Gray squirrels are common in most of the dense, deciduous woods or mixed forests in North America.*

borhood) or stakes and flagging (in the woods). Copy Table 4 into your journal, and use it to keep track of the squirrels' eating and hoarding activity.

When you are ready to leave the site, measure the distance from each stake to the tree under which you spread acorns. Record this data in your journal. If you can get permission from the person who owns the land, leave the stakes in the ground. Return in the spring to see if any of the seeds sprouted.

| Table 4   Monitoring Squirrel Behavior | | | |
|---|---|---|---|
| Activity | Amount of Time Spent on Each Activity | | |
|  | Individual 1 | Individual 2 | Individual 3 | Individual 4 |
| Resting | | | | |
| Eating | | | | |
| Grooming | | | | |
| Foraging | | | | |
| Chasing | | | | |
| Vocalizing | | | | |

Repeat the activity several more times, bringing fresh acorns each time. What is the average distance a squirrel carries a nut before burying it? What is the farthest distance you observed? Some observers have seen squirrels burying seeds up to 30 meters (100 ft.) from the parent tree!

PROJECT **13**

## What Galls You?

Many kinds of insects, mites, bacteria, viruses, fungi, and nematodes stimulate plants to form small growths or swellings to house and feed their developing eggs. These growths, called **galls**, can be found on leaves, buds, flowers, and even woody twigs and stems.

Galls are common and easy to find. With a hand lens, a ruler, a scalpel or single-edged razor blade, and plastic sandwich bags, you can learn quite a lot about these amazing structures.

Visit a nearby wooded area to collect a few galls. What plants should you look for? Although the organisms respon-

*Galls sometimes have shapes that resemble flower parts, leaves, or even fruits, like this oak-apple gall.*

sible for gall formation invade a wide variety of tree species, the oak family is one of their favorites. More than 800 different gall insects and mites infect oak trees. When you find a tree with galls, use a scalpel or a single-edged razor blade to collect several samples of each kind of gall. Write the location and date of collection on each bag.

When you return home or to school, use a hand lens to examine the galls carefully. Sketch each gall in your journal. Be sure to record the overall size and shape. Try to identify the type of gall by consulting a field guide to insects. Look for small holes in the gall's surface. These may be exit holes through which the mature gall insects left.

Now cut the gall open. Make your cut slightly off-center to avoid injuring the larvae inside. How many larvae are there? Describe the internal structure of the gall in your journal.

Beginning in late spring, follow the development of one type of gall. Make weekly trips to collect samples. How long does it take for the larvae to mature? How does the appearance of the gall change over time?

In the fall, collect some galls and a twig from the tree they grow on. When you return home, set up a breeding chamber as shown in Figure 12 on the next page. You will need a large glass jar, a small glass jar, a piece of muslin, a rubber band, and water. Place the leafy twig inside the breeding chamber. Poke a hole in the muslin just large enough for the plant's stem.

Place the jar outside or in the garage through the winter. It may be several months before the larvae hatch, but monitor any changes on a weekly basis. Try to identify the adults using a field guide to insects.

### ✔ Doing More

Many insects spend their time in the boughs and leaves of forest trees. Often they are well camouflaged. To find out what's up there, gather a large white sheet or light-colored umbrella, a hand lens, a hiking stick or broomstick, a **pooter**, forceps, and collecting jars. You can make your own pooter using instructions in the Appendix at the back of this book. Bring along several friends and a field guide to insects.

Ask your friends to hold the sheet or upside-down umbrella below a tree branch. Using the hiking stick or broomstick, rap a tree limb sharply several times. Repeat this procedure under several limbs of the same tree before stop-

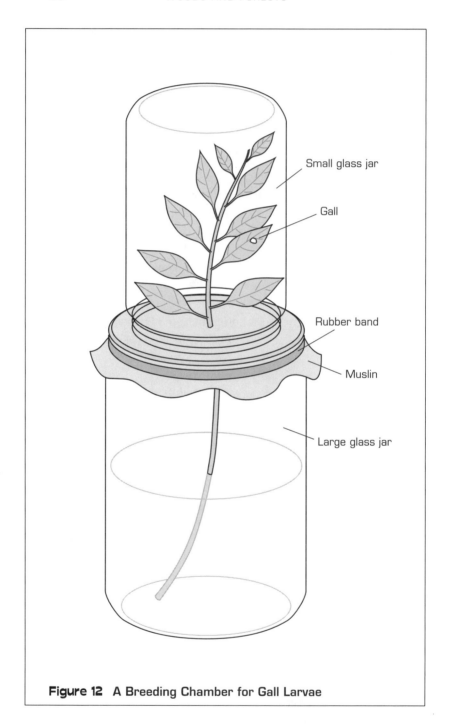

Small glass jar

Gall

Rubber band

Muslin

Large glass jar

**Figure 12**  A Breeding Chamber for Gall Larvae

ping to examine your catch. Use forceps or a pooter to transfer the insects to collecting jars. What creatures can you identify? Examine other trees in the forest. Do some insects seem to prefer certain kinds of trees?

## Animals of the Soil and Critters of the Litter

Grab a handful of forest soil and leaves. Can you guess how many creatures you're now holding? More creatures than the entire human population on Earth! Insects, spiders, and other arthropods live there, but most of the organisms in soil are microscopic.

In nature, size is no indication of importance. Minute soil creatures perform an indispensable service to the forest. By decomposing leaves and woody debris, they recycle essential nutrients back into the soil. The trees, in turn, drop food in the form of leaves and branches, returning favor for favor in this mutualistic relationship.

To explore the world of the forest floor, you'll need resealable plastic bags, a hand lens or dissecting microscope borrowed from your school's science department, a hand trowel, your journal, several white trays or pans, forceps, a Berlese funnel, a pooter, and small collecting jars containing alcohol. Directions for making a pooter and a Berlese funnel are included in the Appendix at the back of this book.

Visit a forest when temperatures are mild, such as early summer or early fall, to survey the small animals that live in the soil and litter. Step off the beaten path or trail to find an undisturbed area. ***Keep an eye out for poison ivy!***

Look closely at the uppermost layer of leaves on the forest floor. Pick up a few leaves and examine them. Record your observations in your journal. With your hands, dig a little deeper to a layer of broken and crumbled leaves. Place pieces in a white pan or tray and sort through the litter.

Do you see tiny white flecks jumping among the leaves? These are springtails, primitive wingless insects that use their spring-loaded tails to propel themselves out of danger. You may also see mites and larger animals, such as pill bugs, ants, spiders, centipedes, millipedes, daddy longlegs, and earthworms. Use a field guide to help you identify the creatures. Continue working your way deeper, noting the types of creatures and the level at which they are living.

Sifting through leaves and soil is tedious work. Sometimes you miss some interesting creatures. Why not let the animals sort themselves? For a more efficient and complete survey, try a clever device called a Berlese funnel. This device uses the heat from an overhead lightbulb to drive creatures in a soil and leaf litter sample through a funnel and into a collecting jar.

Be sure to check your sample often—you may need to reposition the lightbulb. If the bulb is too close, the animals may overheat and die! It may take more than 12 hours to extract all the animals from the soil and litter.

Which type of animal is most abundant in your sample? How many different kinds can you find? Can you identify them using a field guide? Compare soil and litter samples from coniferous woods and deciduous woods. Which creatures are more numerous in each?

# CHAPTER 5

# *Cycles and Flows: Functions of a Forest Ecosystem*

FORESTS AND THE CREATURES THAT live in them have many important jobs. Forests slow the flow of water over the land, protect the soil, and keep rivers and streams running clear. Forest plants use energy from sunlight to make sugars from carbon dioxide and water.

Because plants make their own food, they are called **producers**. The food materials tied up in the bodies of producers are used by a second group of creatures, called **consumers**. A caterpillar feeding on an oak leaf is a consumer, as is a titmouse that eats the caterpillar. If a weasel eats the titmouse, it is a tertiary consumer—third in line along the **food chain**. But this isn't the end of the line. A special class of consumers preys not on the living, but on the

91

*Millions of tiny fungal threads penetrate the wood of a fallen log and begin its decay. The shelf-like structures attached to the bark are the reproductive structures of the fungus.*

dead. These consumers—mostly bacteria, fungi, and insects—are called **decomposers**.

Through the action of decomposers, another major function of the forest comes about—recycling carbon and essential nutrients. Some elements, such as carbon and nitrogen, are necessary for life. If these were used up, all life on Earth would die. Instead, these elements are recycled. Forest plants and soil microbes extract them from the soil or air, using them to make important molecules for growth. Consumers incorporate these molecules into their own bodies. When a plant or animal dies, decomposers release these elements back to the air and soil, to be used again. These cycles are critical to life on Earth.

Water, too, is recycled. Through the processes of evaporation and precipitation, water molecules move between the ocean, the atmosphere, and the land. Water falling on the land seeps into the soil or runs overland, ultimately making its way to a nearby stream or lake. Ridges and valleys in the landscape determine the direction and extent of this flow. The land over which water travels to reach a stream or lake is called a **watershed**.

Forested watersheds intercept rain and snow differently than other land surfaces. Falling water can be trapped by the leaves and bark of forest trees. From there it may evaporate. Or, the water may slowly drip onto the forest floor. Once it has soaked into the ground, the water may be taken up by forest plants and evaporated through their leaves. Water seeping into deeper layers of the soil may be held for some time in underground reservoirs.

The activities in this chapter will help you learn more about the functions of a forest ecosystem, explore forest food chains, the world of the decomposers, and the path water follows through wooded areas.

PROJECT **15**

## Owl Pellets and Animal Scat: Looking at Leftovers

A caterpillar grazes on the leaves of a maple tree. Nearby, a chickadee flits from limb to limb. With one neat swoop, the bird nabs the caterpillar and swallows it. A few minutes later, a dark, streamlined form flying swiftly through the woods sinks its talons into the small bird and carries it away.

Have you ever observed any of these events? Figuring out a forest **food web** can be overwhelming. One way to learn what an animal eats is by looking at what's left over.

Birds of prey, such as owls and hawks, regurgitate their leftovers as small, compact bundles of hair, feathers, bones, and teeth. These regurgitated wads are called pellets. Once or twice a day a pellet is coughed up. Because many owls eat their prey whole, an owl pellet may contain an entire skeleton.

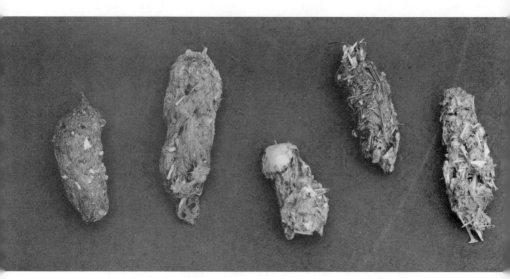

*Owl pellets hold clues to this bird's feeding habits. What bones do you see here?*

To discover what a bird had for dinner last night, collect owl pellets from a nearby wooded area or a barn. If you have trouble finding them, you can order them from one of the biological supply house listed in the For Further Information section at the back of this book. You'll also need forceps, a dissecting needle, a ruler, a small bowl of water, a white tray, a hand lens, and your journal.

First examine the outside of the pellet. Measure it. To see what's inside, soften the pellet by soaking it in water for 30 minutes. Transfer the pellet to a white tray. Pull the pellet apart with forceps and a dissecting needle. Sort everything into the following categories: skulls, jaws and teeth, bones, hair and feathers, and miscellaneous. Group bones of the same kind together. After completely dissecting the pellet, use Figure 13 identify the bones.

Can you tell what kind of animal or animals the owl ate recently? How many did it eat (count the number of skulls)? How varied is the owl's diet?

**Figure 13**  The Bones of a Small Animal

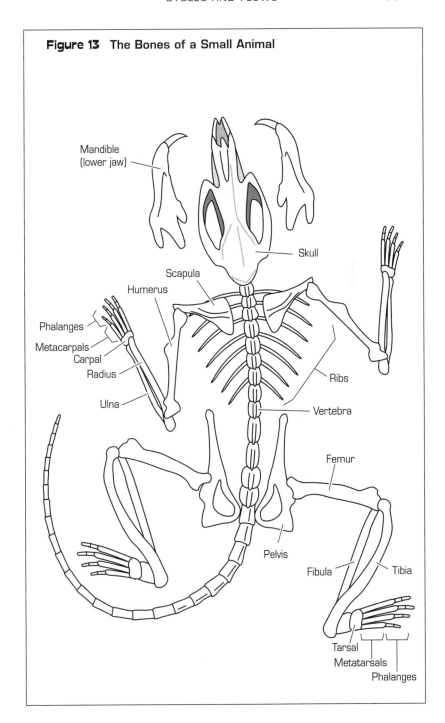

✔ **Doing More**

Try mounting a complete skeleton from one pellet. Glue the bones to foam board or plywood.

Not all animals cough up pellets, but all animals eliminate waste products. While looking at animal scat is not for everyone, you can learn something from it. As you walk through the woods, be on the lookout for scat. Collect samples in small plastic bags and examine them at home. *Be sure to observe commonsense health precautions when handling scat!*

Describe the outer appearance of the scat in your journal, then cut it in half lengthwise and see what's inside. If you want to know what animal the scat came from, refer to a guidebook on animal tracking. A few are listed in the For Further Information section at the back of this book.

PROJECT **16**

# Listening to the Sounds of a Dead Log

Death is often described as cold, still, and silent. A dead log, though, is full of sounds. Inside, animals chew, scrape, and claw tunnels and cavities through the wood. Tiny feet scurry through a multitude of openings. The high-pitched sounds of bessbugs wax and wane.

With some simple tools and a little patience, you can observe life in a dead log firsthand. You'll need forceps, a pooter, small paper cups, index cards, white plastic spoons, collecting jars, a white pan or tray, a hand lens, and your journal. You can make a pooter using instructions in the Appendix at the back of this book. Borrow a stethoscope from your school's science lab. You'll also want a field guide to mushrooms and fungi as well as a field guide to insects and spiders.

Visit a nearby wooded area to look for fallen logs. Choose a log with soft, spongy wood and a surface marked with holes and cavities. Before you disturb the log, use a stethoscope to listen to the activities of the animals inside. Press the diaphragm of the stethoscope directly against the surface of the log. What do you hear? Try listening to sounds in a dead standing tree (a snag) or any tree trunk that shows insect damage.

Now observe a small area along the surface of the dead log. Make notes or sketches in your journal. Peel away the outer layers of the log with forceps. Collect any creatures you may find using a pooter, forceps, a plastic spoon, or a small square of paper and a cup. To use the cup and paper, trap the animal with the cup, then slide the paper underneath. Invert the cup to force the animal to the bottom. Transfer it to a collecting jar.

Look for animals underneath the log by carefully rolling it over. *Do not place your hands underneath the log! Roll it over with your feet. Be sure to wear heavy shoes or boots if poisonous snakes are common in your area. Step back as the log rolls.*

Examine your collection using a hand lens. A field guide will help you identify your finds. Table 5 lists some of the creatures you may encounter. When you have finished with the log, return it to its original position. You may want to take a few specimens with you, but leave the rest where you found them.

**Table 5   Creatures in a Dead Log**

| The Wood Eaters | The Scavengers | The Predators |
|---|---|---|
| Bark beetles | Mites | Spiders |
| Larvae of click beetles | Millipedes | Salamanders |
| Larvae of metallic | Pill bugs | Centipedes |
|    wood borers | Wood roaches | |
| Long horned beetles | Snails | |
| Engraver beetles | Slugs | |
| Bessbugs | Earthworms | |
| Carpenter ants | | |
| Termites | | |

Be sure to describe in your journal any mushrooms or other types of fungi that you find. Fungi are an important group of decomposers. As you pick through the rotting log, look for a tangled mass of white threads. These threads, or hyphae, belong to a fungus. The entire mass of threads is the body, or **mycelium**, of the fungus.

### ✔ Doing More

While it may take 10 years or more for the tree to decay completely, a 6-month study will reveal the changing communities that live in a dead log. Find a recently fallen log in a wooded area near your home. Make a quick sketch of the location in your journal so that you can easily find it again. Visit the site once a week for several months to observe the log and its inhabitants. What creatures are the first to appear? Were they present throughout the study period? Describe the sequence of animals and other life that inhabited the dead log.

INVESTIGATION **11**

# Meet the Garbage Crew

Over a year's time, leaves, branches, and seeds rain down upon the forest floor. The forest floor is a dumping ground. But members of the clean-up crew, too numerous to count and too small to see, readily dispose of the material. Who are the members of this garbage crew? They include bacteria, fungi, algae, and protozoans. Unlike their human counterparts, this garbage crew doesn't haul anything off to a nearby landfill. Instead, the debris is decomposed and recycled on-site.

To watch this crew at work, gather the following supplies: microscope slides, a permanent marker, rubber bands, clear cellophane, a clay flowerpot, scissors, surveyor's flagging or strips of fabric, gallon-size resealable plastic bags, a large microwavable container with a lid, a thermometer, unexposed but developed 35-millimeter color slide film, a hand lens or dissecting microscope, and a slide projector or slide viewer (optional).

Cellophane comes in clear sheets and is used in packaging foods and other products. You can distinguish it from plastics by the way it crinkles and crackles when crushed into a ball. Purchase a roll of color slide film. (Kodachrome is a good brand to use.) Take the film to a camera shop or film lab to have it processed and mounted. Carefully explain your project. Emphasize that the film is unexposed, but you do want it developed!

Soil microbes are decomposers. They break down proteins, sugars, and other molecules. Proteins are carbon- and nitrogen-containing molecules common to all living things. To watch soil decomposers digest proteins, bury most of the developed slides in forest soil. Position the mounted slides vertically so the top edge of each one is flush with the ground. Mark the site with a piece of surveyor's flagging or fabric strips and sketch a rough map in your journal.

After a week, dig up one slide. Carefully wash it with tap water and let it air dry. Hold the slide up to the light, and look for tiny pinpoints of light on the darkened surface. Use a slide viewer or projector to get a better view. Each subsequent day, remove another slide, wash it, and view it.

Each pinhole is a site of protein breakdown. The coating, or emulsion, on the slide film contains protein. Soil bacteria digest the protein, clearing the film.

To be certain that your results are due to the activity of living organisms, set up a control experiment. Return to your woodland site to collect samples of soil in resealable plastic bags. To sterilize the soil, add 2 to 3 centimeters (about 1 in.) of soil to the microwavable container. Cover the container, and microwave it on high for 5 to 10 minutes.

The soil temperature must reach at least 100°C (212°F) to kill the bacteria. Use a thermometer to check the soil temperature. Place the sterile soil in a clay pot and repeat the experiment with the developed slide film. After embedding the slides, moisten the soil. A week or two later, dig up the film and examine it. Do your results surprise you?

You can observe the action of soil microbes on other carbon compounds by sandwiching cellophane between two glass
microscope slides. First rinse the cellophane to remove any
chemicals. Cut a piece of cellophane the size of a microscope
slide. Place the piece between two glass slides. Use rubber
bands to hold the slides together. Bury the slides vertically in
forest soil, as you did the slide film. After several weeks, remove the slides and examine them with a hand lens or dissecting microscope. Look for threadlike strands of fungi
invading the cellophane from the slide edges. Run a control
using sterile soil.

# Chasing Raindrops

The sky darkens as storm clouds gather over the forest. The
wind whips through the trees, sending branches swaying and
leaves dancing. Thunder booms and crackles just before the
clouds let loose a heavy rain. A raindrop's journey to the top
of a forest might take just a few minutes or as long as a half
hour. But where does the water go from there? What hap-
pens to the rain that falls on a forest?

With some simple equipment and a few friends, you can
begin to answer these questions. Ask the cafeteria supervi-
sor at your school to save twenty to thirty institutional-size
steel cans (the net weight of contents should be approximately 3 kilograms or 7 pounds) for you. You'll also need a
compass, a permanent marker, surveyor's flagging or strips
of fabric, a ruler, a hand calculator, and your journal.

Visit a local wooded area to make an initial survey. Look
around for a nearby open area, such as a meadow. You'll
monitor rainfall at two sites—in the woods and in the
meadow. The clearing must be fairly large so rainfall will not
be obstructed by buildings or trees.

Once you've selected your study sites, you're ready to set
up your rain gauges. At home, number the cans consecu-

tively with a permanent marker. Gather up the cans, the compass, the permanent marker, your journal, and a few friends, and head out to your first study site.

At the clearing, spread two to four cans out on the ground away from nearby trees or buildings. In most cases, the cans should be at least 7 paces apart and at least 30 meters (100 ft.) away from objects that might interfere with rain collection. Note the relative position of the cans in your journal.

Now hike to the nearby wooded study site. Space sixteen to twenty-five cans on the ground in a square grid pattern, with each can about seven paces from its neighbors. Use your compass to help you walk the lines of the grid. After you've positioned all the cans, mark the site with flagging or scraps of fabric. Sketch a simple map in your journal to help you locate the area from the trail.

Keep track of weather forecasts for the next few days. After the first rainstorm, check your rain gauges within 24 hours. Measure the depth of water in each can. If you are having trouble reading the water's depth directly off the ruler, try using a dipstick. Read to the wetted line. In your journal, construct a table to record can numbers and water depths.

Calculate the average rainfall at each site by adding all the recorded depths of rain collected at the site during one storm event, and dividing by the total number of cans. How do the two averages compare? Calculate the percent of rain intercepted by the forest using the formula given below.

$$\frac{\text{rainfall (cm) in clearing} - \text{rainfall (cm) in woods}}{\text{rainfall (cm) in clearing}} \times 100$$

## Holding on to the Soil

Rain takes many paths through a forest. It drips off the leaves, seeps into the soil, and flows into streams and rivers.

As the water flows, it carries with it a part of the forest. The water leaches small molecules from the leaves and tries to wash away pieces of the soil. But the forest trees, with their tangled web of roots and root hairs, cling tightly to the soil. With every storm, the battle rages.

To see the positive effects of a forest on soil erosion and stream sediment, try monitoring several streams using a simple cone-shaped device called an Imhoff cone. You can order one of these devices from a supply company listed in the For Further Information section at the back of this book. The holding rack can also be purchased, but try improvising with a large boot or a container stuffed with newspaper.

Locate streams that drain watersheds where the following land uses predominate: a forest (with few roads), a clearcut or recently logged forest, a field, and a construction site. Ask your parents or other adults in your community to help you find these places. You may also want to consult a highway map or a topographic map.

Once you have pinpointed these different areas on a map, visit each stream. Look for an access point just downstream from each type of land area. If the stream runs through private property, you must obtain the landowner's permission to walk on the property! Bridges or canoe launch points are good spots to get access to the water.

To monitor sediment levels, fill the Imhoff cone with stream water. *Be careful! Never step into a stream without knowing its depth and flow. Currents can be strong, and the water could be deeper than it appears! Most water samples can be taken from the stream bank.*

Set the cone upright, allowing the materials to settle for 45 minutes. At the end of that period, grasp the cone with the palms of both hands and briskly roll it back and forth three times. This knocks loose any sediment that may have adhered to the sides of the cone. Let the material settle for an additional 15 minutes. Read the markings on the side of the cone to record the volume of matter that settles per liter of water.

How do sediment levels from the different streams compare? Which shows the least amount of sediment? Which shows the most? What is the effect of logging on soil erosion and stream sediment levels? How might increased stream sediment affect the creatures that live in the stream?

### ✔ Doing More

Monitor a stream during or immediately after a rain. ***Be careful of rising, fast-flowing water and slippery banks! Ask an adult accompany you.*** Compare sediment levels before, during, and after a storm. Which types of watersheds retain the most soil during a storm?

# CHAPTER 6

# The Future of Our Forests

EVEN AT MIDDAY, THE WOODS WERE quiet and dark. Massive trunks 1 meter (3.3 ft.) or more in diameter stood like silent sentinels. Thirty meters (100 ft.) above the forest floor, a dense canopy topped the forest. The trees held even their lowest branches more than 20 meters (65 ft.) above the ground. The oaks, sugar maples, and chestnuts that dominated these woods were old—400 years or more! Little undergrowth could survive in the perpetual shade. During the day, the woods seemed still and devoid of animal life. Yet, at night, the woods were suddenly alive with creatures. Wolves howled in the distance, while horned owls and whip-poorwills called to each other.

This was the forest that greeted America's settlers and pioneers more than 300 years ago. Almost all woods like this are gone now. As the settlers moved in, they cleared the land for farms and towns. In the 1800s and early 1900s, timber companies cut the trees for lumber. Today, less than one-third of North America is covered by forests. Most of those that remain have been cut one or more times. Less than 5 percent of today's forested lands are **old-growth forests** that have never been touched by an axe or chainsaw.

Driven by our ever-increasing need for lumber and paper products, the felling of the trees continues. But it's not just the loss of trees that's a problem. In many areas, logging practices such as clear-cutting damage the soil and wildlife. Chemicals used to control the regrowth of undesirable plants in the cut-over areas pollute soils and waterways. Forest soils are compacted as large machines scour the land and remove logs. As rain and snowmelt wash over the clear-cut areas, the flowing water carries the soil away, dumping it into nearby streams and choking aquatic life.

These timbering practices are not the only threats to our forests. Other concerns loom just as large. Rising levels of air pollutants are damaging certain forest plants, especially on mountaintops and ridges. Tree growth in some forests has dropped significantly in recent years. Rain polluted by chemicals in the air, or acid rain, appears to be weakening many trees, making them susceptible to insects, fungi, and other agents of disease. Where do these pollutants come from? Most are produced when the chemicals released from car exhaust and smokestacks react with sunlight and air.

Other problems arise when large tracts of forest are carved into smaller and smaller parcels by the sprawling development of our cities and towns. Some animals need large spaces to hunt prey. If these animals are confined to small areas, they will die. Many of our natural forests are being replaced with tree farms and plantations. These extensive farms of trees all the same age and species cannot support the diversity of living things found in old-growth forests. For these reasons, forest creatures such as the spotted owl and grizzly bear are dying off. They are endangered species.

What's being done to protect the forests of North America? What can you do to help? As consumers of forest products and future voting citizens, you can do a lot! Use the activities in this chapter to find out how you can make a difference.

## Making Paper from Yesterday's Notes: The Importance of Recycling

Do you know how much paper or paper products you use in a day, or even a week? Most of the paper we use is made from wood. Some expensive papers are made from hemp and other plant fibers. But notebook paper, photocopy paper, printer paper, and newspaper is usually made from trees. In 1995, Americans used an average of 320 kilograms (700 lbs.) of paper per person—enough to destroy about 0.4 ha. (1 acre) of forest. Most of this paper will wind up in our landfills.

Save a tree—recycle your paper! While you'll want to take most of your wastepaper to a recycling center, it's fun to learn how to recycle your own. You'll need a blender, a large jar, five sheets of used white paper (standard letter size), liquid laundry starch, a teaspoon, water, a serving spoon, a bucket or other large plastic container, a rolling pin, wax paper, and a window screen. Look for liquid laundry starch at your local grocery or discount store.

Tear the paper into pieces the size of a dime or smaller. Soak the paper shreds in very hot water for 30 minutes. As the water cools, fill a blender half full of warm water. Add several spoonfuls of shredded paper and one teaspoon of liquid laundry starch to the blender. Blend until the mixture is thick and pulpy.

While standing over the kitchen sink, pour the mixture over the window screening. ***Do not pour any leftover pulp down the drain! It may clog your pipes.*** Use your hands to spread the pulp evenly across the screen. Form the mixture into whatever size and shape you want. Cover the pulp with a sheet of wax paper. Use a rolling pin to press the pulp into a smooth sheet.

Carefully turn the screen over and peel the flattened pulp off the screen onto a flat, smooth surface. Allow it to dry in the sun.

### ✔ Doing More

Reduce your need for paper products. For example, use cloth towels or rags instead of paper towels, dishware rather than paper plates, and cloth napkins in place of paper napkins. Pack your groceries in recyclable plastic bags or reusable canvas bags.

When you buy paper, look for products with at least 50 percent postconsumer waste. Check with organizations like Co-op America or America Recycles Day for other ways to cut back on paper waste. The Web addresses of these groups are listed in the For Further Information section at the back of this book.

**INVESTIGATION  13**

# Monitoring for Acid Rain

When coal, oil, and gasoline are burned, pollutants are released into the atmosphere. When the pollutants react with tiny water droplets high in the clouds, the water becomes acidic and falls to Earth as acid precipitation. Acid rain and snow can harm the plants and animals that live in forests, rivers, and lakes.

Acids are chemicals with lots of free, or unattached, positively charged hydrogen ions ($H^+$). A special scale, called the **pH** scale, is used to describe the concentration of these ions in a solution. The units range from 0 to 14. Acidic solutions register below 7 on the pH scale. Solutions with a pH of 7 are neutral, while solutions with a pH greater than 7 are basic.

How much acid is in the rain that falls where you live? To find out, you'll need several rain gauges (see Investigation 12), a map of North America, collecting jars, a permanent marker, and a good quality pH paper or a pH meter. The science supply companies listed in the For Further Information section at the back of this book sell pH paper. If you borrow a pH meter, ask your science teacher to show you how to use it. ***Be very careful with the glass probe or electrode. The tip breaks easily!***

To monitor the acidity of the rainfall in your area, set up several rain gauges. Make sure the gauges are clean and mount each one on a pole or in the ground—well away from any overhead trees or buildings. Number each rain gauge and note its location in your journal.

Keep track of the weather forecast for your area. When you hear that a storm is on its way, find out the direction from which it is approaching. Has it passed through any major cities? Make a list of this information in your journal.

After the storm has passed, collect the rain from each gauge. Measure the pH of each sample and record the results in your journal. If you're using pH paper, dip one end of a fresh paper strip in each sample. After a few seconds, pull it out and compare the color of the paper to the color chart that came with the pH paper. Acid rain has a pH of less than 5.6. The lowest pH of any rain ever collected and tested was less than 2.0! Compare the pH of rain collected from different storms. Can you correlate the pH with the route of the storm?

## ✔ Doing More

To reduce air pollution and acid rain, conserve energy at home and school. Use appliances that are energy efficient. Ride your bike, walk, carpool, or ride the bus whenever possible! For other tips, check out the EPA's Acid Rain Program Web site. The address is listed in the For Further Information section at the back of this book.

## Plant a Tree, Grow a Forest

Millions of acres of North American forests have been lost since the turn of the century. Additional acres of forest have suffered from the effects of clear-cutting, insect pests, and acid precipitation. While restoring those ecosystems might seem impossible, it can start with the simple act of planting a tree. Even if you're not involved in a large-scale project, plant a tree! Each tree that's planted benefits Earth.

You don't need a lot of special equipment or a green thumb to successfully plant a tree. Trees can be planted in the spring or fall. You'll need a tree seedling or sapling, a shovel, a meterstick, mulch, and a watering can or garden hose attached to an outside spicket. Mulch can be purchased at a nursery or garden supply store. Pine bark or wood chips are good mulches to use. Grass clippings will work, too. A clean, 20-liter (5-gal.) paint bucket with small holes poked in the bottom can be used instead of a watering can.

If you want to plant a tree in your own yard, discuss the idea with your parents. Agree on a site for the new tree, then take a trip to a reputable nursery. Seek the advice of the nursery staff. They can tell you which trees are well suited to the conditions of your site.

To save money, purchase seedlings. Keep your eyes open for plant sales in the spring or fall. Often scout troops, garden clubs, or nature centers will hold plant sales to raise money. Check them out for healthy tree seedlings at a reasonable price. Once you've made your purchase, store your tree in a cool, shady spot until you're ready to plant it.

Before you begin digging, measure the roots of the tree. If you've purchased a tree wrapped in burlap or in a container, simply measure the size of the root ball (depth and width) or container. For a seedling, measure from the lowest point on the trunk to the tip of the longest main root.

Remove the grass from the planting site and discard it. Begin digging. Rely on the measurements you took of the root system to determine the size of the hole you need to dig. Check the depth of the hole periodically with a meterstick. You'll want a hole just deep enough to allow the top of the root ball or root system to rest at the soil surface when planted. Make the hole wider than the roots so they will have room to spread out.

When the hole is the right size, set the tree down in it. Loosen, but do not remove, the burlap from a tree with a wrapped root ball. Before filling the hole with dirt, make sure the tree isn't leaning. Fill in the hole with the dirt you removed. Break apart any large clumps of soil. If you're planting a seedling, support it with your hands as you fill in the hole. Keep the main root straight—a seedling with a U-shaped root will likely die. Pack the soil firmly with your hands or feet.

Soak the newly packed soil with water, then spread mulch to a depth of 5 to 10 centimeters (2 to 4 in.). Keep the mulch a few centimeters (1 to 2 in.) back from trunk of the tree. Mulch helps the soil retain moisture and insulates the roots from excessive temperatures. Arrange the mulch into the shape of a shallow bowl, so it forms a water-holding basin.

As a general rule, you should water your tree once a week. Of course, if the weather is unusually dry or wet, you'll need to adjust to these conditions. If you use a hose, let the water trickle very slowly. Better yet, fill a 20-liter (5-gal.) bucket with small holes in the bottom, and set it next to the tree. You'll have little problem with surface runoff.

Monitor your tree closely for the first year after planting. Watch for signs of disease and insect or animal pests. Consult your local nursery staff if you suspect problems.

To organize a tree-planting event or get involved with a reforestation project, contact these organizations for more information: the National Arbor Day Foundation, American Forests (Global ReLeaf Program), and the United States Forest Service. You can contact these groups using information listed in the For Further Information section at the back of this book.

# How to Write a Letter and Save a Forest!

America's forests need your help. But you don't have to tramp through the woods or dig in the dirt to make a difference. All you need to do is sit down and write a letter! Many of the forests in this country are on public lands—lands managed by the United States Forest Service or the Bureau of Land Management.

Decisions about how to manage these forests are ultimately controlled by Congress and the president of the United States. As officials elected by the public, they need and want to hear from people like you and me.

You can influence these people in many ways. One way is to write a letter stating your views on a particular problem or issue. All you need is a pen or pencil, several sheets of notebook paper or typing paper, a business envelope, a first-class postage stamp, and the telephone directory. The blue pages of your local phone book lists local, state, and federal government agencies and departments. Use it to find the names of your senator or representative.

Who should you write to? How do you find their names and addresses? If you're concerned about an issue relating to our national forests, contact your U.S. senator or representative. If you like going straight to the top, write to the president! The following addresses may come in handy.

President (use full name)
The White House
1600 Pennsylvania Avenue
Washington, DC 20500

Senator (use full name)
United States Senate
Washington, DC 20510

Representative (use full name)
House of Representatives
Washington, DC 20515

Director Michael Dombeck
United States Forest Service
Department of Agriculture
P.O. Box 96090
Washington, DC 20090

Acting Director Tom Fry
Bureau of Land Management
1849 C Street, NW
Washington, DC 20240

What should you write about? Debates and issues regarding forests abound these days. Here are a few examples:

- Federal subsidies to the timber industry.
- Damaging effects of clear-cutting.
- Construction of new roads by the Forest Service, especially in areas designed as Wilderness Areas.
- Effects of acid precipitation, acid deposition, and other forms of air pollution on forests, especially in the Great Smoky Mountains National Park—one of the United States's most heavily visited parks.
- Legislation to limit air pollutants derived from the combustion of fossil fuels.
- The continuing destruction of old-growth forests of the Pacific Northwest, including the Tongass National Forest in Alaska.
- Legislation to create old-growth forest reserves.
- State versus federal control of log exports.
- Rapid deforestation of the world's rain forests.

Before you write, get informed about the issue you decide to tackle. Contact Save America's Forests, the Nature Conservancy, or the Sierra Club for advice and information. See the For Further Information section at the back of this book for their addresses.

When you do write, focus on one issue per letter. The body of the letter should be no longer than a page. Remember the acronym KISS—Keep It Short and Simple. State your point of view and explain what action or actions you'd like to see taken. Mention your school name and grade in your letter.

Once you have a rough draft, let your teacher or parent read it over. Make a final copy using the accepted style for a business letter. Put the letter in an envelope, address the envelope (be sure to include a return address), add a postage stamp, and mail it!

# *Conclusion*

FORESTS ARE SPECIAL PLACES. WHEN you step inside a forest, you feel like you've entered a secret world—one far removed from the human world. Yet forests are vital ecosystems. We depend on the important jobs they do. As you performed the projects and investigations in this book, you explored a few of their functions. You explored their role as primary food producers and regulators of water flow, their impact on carbon and nutrient cycles, and their role in modifying local conditions and creating homes for wildlife.

Like all plants, forest plants are producers. They make their own food, and they serve as food for consumers. Many of the consumers that eat plants are preyed on by other consumers. Decomposers that live in forest soils break down the tissues of dead plants and animals. By releasing carbon and nutrients such as nitrogen back to the air or soil, they recycle these important substances. Forest plants cycle carbon by extracting carbon dioxide from the air, using it to make sugars. By removing a greenhouse gas, healthy forests may act as buffers against the agents of global warming.

The carbon and nutrient cycles are not the only cycles affected by forests. Forests play an important role in regulating the movement of water that falls. Bare, hard soil is readily washed away by the pounding effects of rain. In a forest, though, leaves, branches, and stems soften the impact. A carpet of dead leaves protects the soil. Below ground, roots cling to soil particles. From the leaves and branches, water drips and trickles slowly to the ground, seeping into the spongy forest floor. By slowing overland water flow, forests reduce soil erosion. Soil particles that end up in rivers and streams kill aquatic life and pollute our drinking water.

Forests change the air and soil in other ways, too. Forest trees provide shade, cooling the air and soil. Trees release water vapor through their leaves, humidifying the air. Trees block the wind, providing protection and lessening water loss. Trees drop leaves and branches to the ground, protecting the soil and providing food for many creatures. Beneath the ground tree roots loosen the soil, letting in air and water. Forest trees also create habitats for an amazing diversity of living things.

We are only now beginning to understand the many benefits that forests provide. You can help protect our precious forests. Use the knowledge and experience you've gained from the activities and information presented in this book. Get involved. Make a difference.

# *Tools and Equipment*

Even without any special equipment or tools, a walk in the woods can be a pleasant experience. But why settle for just pleasant? Have an adventure! Be an explorer! With just a few of the following devices and supplies, you can turn a ho-hum walk into an adventure. Consider taking along some of the following items the next time you go into the woods.

- binoculars
- a hand lens or magnifying glass
- a hand trowel or small shovel
- collecting jars, plastic sandwich bags, and garbage bags
- forceps
- surveyor's flagging or strips of fabric (bright colors only)
- a 15-centimeter (6-in.) ruler and 7.5-meter (25-ft.) tape measure
- a compass
- white plastic or white enamel pans or trays
- pruning shears or an old pair of scissors
- preserving fluid (ethanol or rubbing alcohol)

The following equipment can be constructed from materials you may already have at home. Add these pieces to your bag of tricks as you seek to uncover the hidden life of the forest.

## Berlese Funnel

Picking through soil and leaf litter to search for tiny critters is tedious and time-consuming. With a Berlese funnel you can let the animals sort themselves right into your collecting jar! To make this device, you'll need a large (2-quart) funnel, a small plastic collecting jar, hardware cloth, a ringstand with a ring and clamp, wire cutters, a ruler, a 40-watt lightbulb, and a gooseneck or swing-arm desk lamp. Check for large funnels wherever automotive supplies are sold. Hardware cloth is a wire mesh with a large mesh size. It is usually sold at hardware stores, farm supply shops, and home building supply stores.

To hold the funnel upright, use a ring stand, ring, and clamp borrowed from your school's science lab. Find a table or desktop on which to assemble the funnel. Set up the desk lamp. Before plugging it into an electric outlet, remove the bulb and replace it with a 40-watt bulb. Place the ring stand underneath the desk lamp. Place the funnel in the opening of the ring.

Slide a collecting jar up underneath the spout of the funnel. With wire cutters, cut a 7.5-centimeter (3-in.) diameter circle from the hardware cloth. Set the hardware cloth inside the funnel so that it blocks the opening leading to the spout. Center the head of the desk lamp over the top of the funnel. See Figure 14 on the next page.

To use the funnel, place a handful of leaf litter and soil in the funnel. Turn the desk lamp on and position the bulb about 15 centimeters (6 in.) above the top of the litter. The heat from the bulb will drive the creatures deeper into the funnel. Eventually they will fall through the spout and be trapped in the collecting jar below.

It may take a day or longer to completely extract the creatures from your litter sample. Check your apparatus periodically. If set up improperly, it could be a fire hazard! If the top layer of leaves feels too hot after an hour or so, move the bulb farther away.

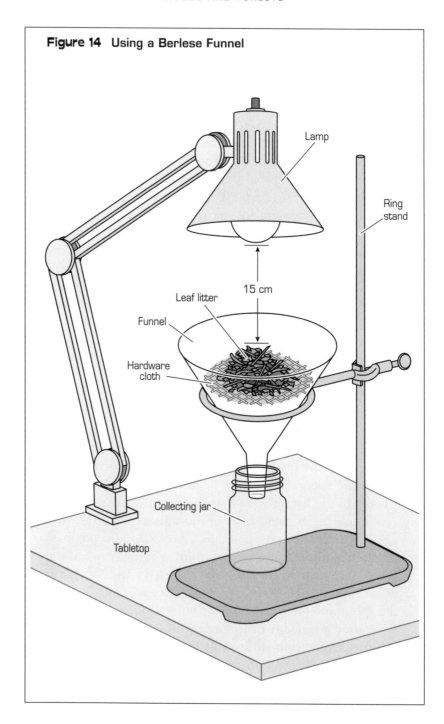

**Figure 14** Using a Berlese Funnel

For a permanent collection of soil and litter animals, fill the collection jar with preserving fluid before placing a sample in the funnel.

## Chalk Bag

In your surveys of the woods, you may find yourself counting trees and identifying species. To keep from losing track, use a chalk bag to mark each tree. Chalk isn't harmful and it washes away easily. To make a chalk bag, you will need sidewalk chalk and a rolling pin. Ask your mom or dad for a couple of old socks—the bigger, the better!

To make the bag, select two or three pieces of white sidewalk chalk. Put them inside the sock and tie off the open end. Use the rolling pin to break the chalk into a powder.

To use the chalk bag, just slap it against the trunk of a tree. The bag will leave a chalk mark that should be easy to spot. You may want to make up several bags, each containing chalk of a different color. Test each bag on a tree in your yard or neighborhood before heading into the woods. Some colors may be easier to see than others.

## Clinometer

It is very difficult to measure the height of a tree directly, so people often rely on mathematical relationships between triangles. Luckily, you don't have to be a mathematical wizard to do this. You can use a homemade device called a clinometer. You'll need a protractor, a 20-centimeter (8-in.) piece of string, a drinking straw, clear packing tape, scissors or a utility knife, and a fishing weight or large nut. Protractors can be found wherever school supplies are sold. Look for one that is at least 15 centimeters (6 in.) along the straight edge.

Tie one end of the string to the weight, and loop the other through the hole in the protractor. To make a sight-

## Figure 15  Making and Using a Clinometer

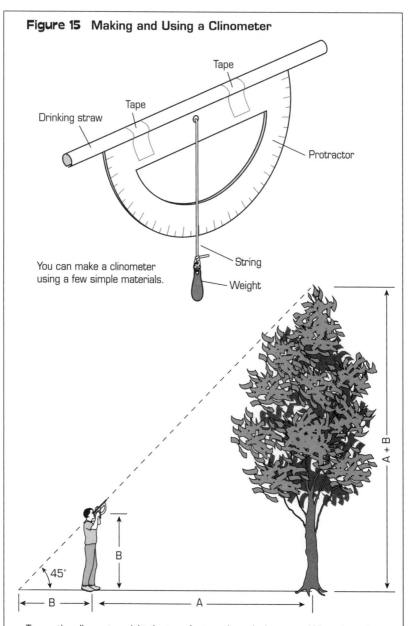

You can make a clinometer using a few simple materials.

To use the clinometer, sight the top of a tree through the straw. When the string crosses 45° mark on the protractor, ask your friend to measure the distance between you and the tree and the distance from your eye to the ground. If you add these distances, you can determine the height of the tree.

ing tube, cut along the length of the drinking straw. Slide the straw down the straight edge of the protractor. Before taping the straw in position, adjust it so you can see through it. See Figure 15.

To use your clinometer, you'll need a friend to assist you, as well as a tape measure that is at least 7.5 meters (25 ft.) long. Practice measuring the height of a flagpole, a telephone pole, a street lamp, or a backyard tree. Stand 6 to 9 meters (20 to 30 ft.) from the object. Hold the clinometer a few inches away from your face so that, by squinting one eye, you can sight through the straw with your other eye. Tilt the protractor until the top of the object is in your line of sight. See Figure 15.

Have your friend read the angle on the protractor where the weighted string crosses the scale. Keep your sight focused on the top of the object as you move a few steps backward or forward until the weighted string crosses the 45° mark of the clinometer. Remain at that spot while your friend measures the distance from you to the object and the distance from the ground to eye level. To determine the height of the object, add the two measurements.

Now try measuring the height of a tree in a nearby woods. You'll find it a little more difficult, but with practice it gets easier. Avoid trees that lean excessively and try to work in a level area.

## Diameter Tape

Scientists and foresters often compare trees by measuring the diameter of their trunks at breast height (DBH)—1.5 meters (4.5 ft.) above the ground. While you can use an ordinary tape measure to measure the distance around the trunk (the circumference) and then calculate the diameter using the equation diameter = circumference/3.14, most foresters use a diameter tape. Diameter tapes are premarked in distances equivalent to trunk diameter. Reading the markings on the tape will give you the diameter directly without having to do extra calculations.

A diameter tape is easy to make. You will need a fastener hook, a needle and thread, a stapler and staples, a permanent marker, a ruler, and three cloth tailor's tape measures (look for ones with markings on one side only). You can find this type of tape measure at fabric stores or discount stores that carry sewing supplies. Look for fastener hooks at a home building supply store or a hardware store.

Using the needle and thread, attach the fastener hook to one end of the tailor's tape measure. Staple and sew the second tape measure to the other end of the first tape measure. The unmarked sides of each tape measure should face in the same direction. Next, attach the third tape measure to the second one.

Using a ruler and a permanent marker, draw a line down the length of the tape measures, making a cross mark every 3.14 centimeters for a metric diameter tape (or $3\frac{1}{8}$ in. for an English tape). Now go back and number each cross mark consecutively from the hook end. Be sure to write the appropriate units (centimeters or inches) several times along the length of the tape measures.

To use the diameter tape, push the hook into the bark of a tree trunk. Run the rest of the tape around the trunk at a height of 1.5 meters (4.5 ft.). Try to keep the tape level all the way around the trunk.

## Extendible Pole

An extendible pole can come in handy when investigating climatic factors high above your head. When marked appropriately, it can also be used to measure the heights of trees in the understory.

To make such a pole, purchase the following materials: a 10-foot length of polyvinylchloride (PVC) piping that is $1\frac{1}{2}$ inches in diameter, a 10-foot length of PVC piping that is 2-inches in diameter, a $1\frac{1}{2}$-inch PVC coupling, a 2-inch coupling, and a 2- to $1\frac{1}{2}$-inch reducer. You'll also need a small eyelet or hook, black electrical tape, black 1-inch stick-on numbers and letters, a tape measure, a pencil, a drill and drill bits, and a hacksaw with a metal-cutting blade.

To add a small platform to the top of the pole, you will need a 6-inch length of PVC piping that is 1 inch in diameter, a metal binding clip (from an office supply store), a 6-inch square piece of foam board or corrugated cardboard, hot glue, and a hot glue gun. You can find these materials at most home building supply stores or hardware stores. Stick-on letters and numbers are sold at art and drafting supply shops.

Using a pencil and measuring tape, mark the midpoint of each 10-foot section of PVC piping. Saw each piece in half using a hacksaw with a metal-cutting blade.

Assemble the pole using the couplings to connect two 5-foot pieces of the same diameter and the reducers to connect two pieces of different diameters. See Figure 16 on the next page. About 7 inches from the top of the pole, drill a small hole to place a screw eye or small hook. Use a drill bit slightly smaller than the diameter of the threads on the screw eye or hook. This can serve as a place to attach a thermometer.

To construct a platform to hold a light meter or Solargraphics paper, hot glue a 6-inch square of cardboard or foam board to one end of a 6-inch length PVC piping that is 1-inch in diameter. Slip the piping down into the top of the pole. Use a metal binding clip to attach the instrument or paper to the platform.

To use the pole for estimating heights, place a thin strip of black electrical tape every 10 centimeters along the length of the pole. Place double strips of tape at 1-meter intervals, and add stick-on numbers to indicate the height.

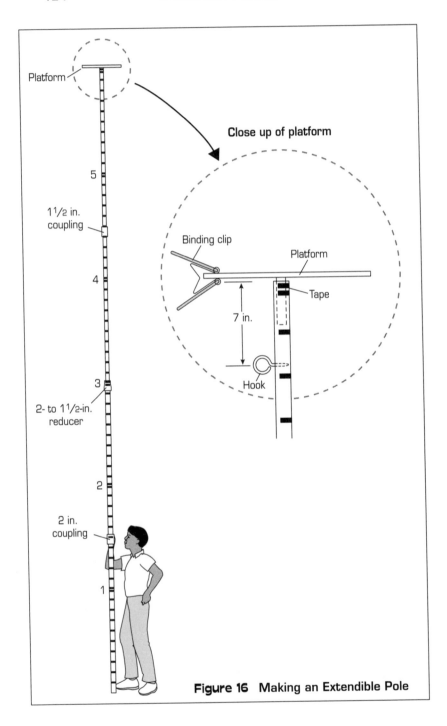

Platform

5

1¹/₂ in.
coupling

4

3

2- to 1¹/₂-in.
reducer

2

2 in.
coupling

1

**Close up of platform**

Binding clip

Platform

Tape

7 in.

Hook

**Figure 16**  Making an Extendible Pole

When not in use, the pole can be broken down into 5-foot (1.5-m) pieces. Use rubber bands to keep the lengths together. Store the couplers and reducers in a small plastic bag.

## Plant Press

As you explore the woods, you may wish to begin a collection of unusual plants you come across. To preserve your specimens, you can press them between the pages of a telephone book. Stack several heavy books on top. After a week or two, your plant samples will be pressed and dried.

If you plan on beginning a serious collection, use a plant press. Your specimens will be better preserved and ready for mounting. To make your own press, you'll need a power saw, scissors, a utility knife, a pencil, a meterstick, two 45 × 30 centimeter (18 × 12 in.) sheets of plywood that are 6 mm ($\frac{1}{4}$ in.) thick, two 1.5-cm ($\frac{5}{8}$ -in.) straps with metal buckles 132-cm (52-in.) long, corrugated cardboard, blotting paper, and several newspapers.

The straps can be purchased from a camping or hiking supplier. Ask for discarded cardboard boxes at your local grocery store or appliance store. Blotting paper is sold at office supply stores. You may substitute watercolor paper. You'll need enough cardboard to cut between five and ten 30 × 45 centimeter (12 × 18 in.) pieces and enough blotting paper to cut twenty pieces of the same size.

With scissors or a utility knife, cut the blotting paper and corrugated cardboard. Use the scissors to trim at least five folded newspaper sheets to the same size as the cardboard and blotting papers. *If you are using a utility knife, be very careful. The blade is razor sharp!* The cardboard pieces will act as ventilators, allowing air to circulate through the plant material. This speeds up the drying process and results in better preserved specimens.

Use a power saw to cut the plywood sheets to the size indicated. *If you have never used this tool before, ask an adult to assist you.* Some home building supply stores or hardware stores may be willing to cut the wood for you.

To assemble the press, place a piece of cardboard on top of a sheet of plywood. Next, add two blotters followed by a sheet of folded newspaper. Add another two sheets of blotting paper, and then a piece of cardboard. Repeat the same arrangement of layers until you run out of cardboard. When you've placed the last piece of cardboard on the stack, top it with the remaining piece of plywood.

Once you have constructed the press, place one plant specimen in each newspaper folder. Be sure to include an identification number that corresponds to site and collection information recorded in your journal. When pressing leaves, include several leaves as well as a short section of the twig. Wildflower specimens should include leaves and roots.

Loop the two canvas straps around each end of the press. Tighten the straps to apply pressure. Place the press near a heat source or in warm spot to facilitate drying. After 24 hours, replace the newspaper sheets and any blotters that appear damp or discolored. Continue pressing the specimens. Replace the blotting papers and newspaper sheets every 2 to 3 days for a 10-day period (blotting papers can be dried and reused). At the end of this period, the specimens should be completely dry and ready to mount.

Botanists typically mount their specimens on $29 \times 42$ centimeter ($11\frac{1}{2} \times 16\frac{1}{2}$ in.) heavy white herbarium paper. Sheets of thin cardboard will work as well. Herbarium paper can be ordered from biological suppliers (see the For Further Information section at the back of this book). Use white glue to attach the plant specimen to the paper.

Attach a small index card at the lower right corner of each sheet, stating the following information: name of the plant (common name and scientific name), name of collector, date, and location where specimen was collected. Store mounted sheets in large boxes in a dry place.

# Pooter

Imagine an insect the size of a pepper grain that flips itself in the air at the slightest disturbance. How can you pick it up? The best way to capture a tiny creature like a springtail is to use a simple piece of equipment called a pooter.

You can make a pooter from a plastic jar with a lid (a peanut butter jar works well), airline aquarium tubing, a drill with a $\frac{7}{32}$-inch drill bit, scissors, a small square of cheesecloth, a rubber band, hot glue and a glue gun, and a piece of scrap lumber.

Cut two pieces of aquarium tubing. One should be 66 centimeters (26 in.) long and the other should be 25 centimeters (10 in.) long. Next, drill two holes in the jar lid using a $\frac{7}{32}$-inch drill bit. To prevent the lid from cracking, turn it upside down and back it with a scrap wood while drilling. The holes should be about 4 centimeters $(1\frac{1}{2}$ in.) apart.

Begin assembling the pooter by screwing the lid onto the jar. Slide the longest piece of tubing through one hole, until its end is about 1 centimeter $(\frac{1}{2}$ in.) from the bottom of the jar. Slide the shorter piece of tubing into the second hole so that only 2 to 3 centimeters (1 in.) protrude into the jar. See Figure 17 on the next page. Glue the pieces of tubing in place using a hot glue gun. Remove the jar's lid and seal the tubing on the undersurface of the lid using hot glue.

The shorter piece of tubing will act as the mouthpiece; the longer piece will act as the collecting tube. By sucking through the mouthpiece when the jar is sealed, insects can be pulled into the jar through the longer piece of tubing. To prevent insects from being sucked into your mouth, wrap a small piece of cheesecloth around the end of the mouthpiece that's inside the collecting jar. Use a rubber band to hold the cheesecloth in place.

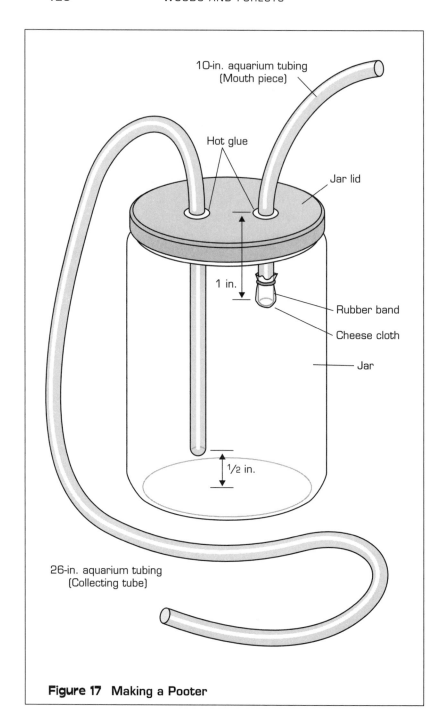

**Figure 17** Making a Pooter

# Throw Rope

A forest is tall. The woods in your area might stand 18 to 24 meters (60 to 80 ft.) tall, while a rain forest canopy can be 30 meters (100 ft.) or more above Earth's surface. Some scientists don special climbing gear to get to the top, but you can begin to investigate what lies over your head with a simple piece of equipment—a throw rope. Whether you're trying to hoist a thermometer into the canopy, or just trying to glimpse a few leaves and twigs, a simple throw rope could be the answer.

To make one, you'll need 15 meters (48 ft.) of light-weight 3-millimeter ($\frac{1}{8}$-in.) cord, a sock, a measuring cup or spoon, and dried beans or rice. Using the measuring cup or spoon, add dried beans or rice to the sock until the foot portion is about half full. Make a knot in the open end of the sock. Just below the knot, securely tie one end of the cord. Check your knots to make sure they won't slip. Keep the cord tangle-free when storing it.

To use this device, simply toss the sock over a branch, letting the cord reel itself out. Pull on both pieces of rope to bend a branch closer to the ground. To hoist an instrument, attach it to the free end of the cord, and pull the sock end toward the ground

# Glossary

**allelopathy**—the inhibition of one plant by another through the release of chemicals

**annual ring**—a concentric ring of wood formed during a single growing season, seen in trees that exhibit a period of growth followed by a dormant period

**bud**—a cluster of cells located along the length of a twig or shoot that is capable of dividing and producing shoots, leaves, or flowers; usually protected by young leaves or scales

**canopy**—the upper layer of a forest formed by the crowns of the tallest forest trees; also called the overstory

**climax community**—the final stage in succession; in the absence of disturbances, this community will persist

**commensalism**—an interaction between two species that live together in which one benefits from the association, while the other is not significantly affected

**coniferous**—a tree that bears cones and does not shed its leaves in the winter

**consumer**—a living organism that is unable to make its own food from nonliving sources, relying instead on energy stored in other living things

**control group**—in an experiment, a group that serves as a standard of comparison to another group that is identical in all respects but one

**crown**—the spread of branches, twigs, and leaves that tops the trunk of a tree

**deciduous**—a plant that sheds its leaves within a short period of time, usually during one season of the year

**decomposer**—an organism capable of breaking down the tissues of dead plants and animals

**ecologist**—a scientist who studies some aspect of ecology, or how living things interact with all aspects of their physical and biological environment

**ecosystem**—a distinct, self-supporting unit of interacting organisms and their environment

**flagellum** (pl. **flagella**)—a long, hairlike organ capable of rotary or whiplike motion; functions in locomotion and feeding

**food chain**—a group of animals that pass energy through a habitat by feeding upon one another

**food web**—a group of living organisms linked by their feeding relationships

**gall**—a tumorlike plant growth that is the result of an interaction between an insect and the tissues of the plant; the gall often houses the larval form of the insect

**germinate**—to sprout; to begin to grow

**hardwood**—the wood produced by a group of flowering trees, including oaks, balsas, mahoganies, and maples

**horizon**—a layer of soil that differs from the soil above and below it by its color, texture, or other properties

**humus**—decomposing plant and animal matter present in the soil

**hybrid**—the offspring of parents of two different varieties or species

**hyphae**—the filaments that make up the body of a fungus

**incubate**—to place a sample in an optimal situation for growth and development

**key**—a special list or arrangement of the defining features of a group of organisms created to assist in the identification and classification of members of the group

**mutualism**—a close association between two living things that benefits both

**mycelium**—the mass of hyphae that forms the body of a fungus

**old-growth forest**—a forest that features fallen, decaying logs, a mix of old and young trees, gaps in the canopy, dead standing trees, a tremendous diversity of plant life, and little or no disturbance from logging; a structurally complex forest that has not been directly altered by humans

**pH**—a measure of the relative acidity, or concentration of hydrogen ions, of a substance; based on a scale of 0 to 14 where 0 is the most acidic and 14 is least acidic or most basic

**phloem**—the tissue found in most land plants that conducts sugars and other foodstuffs throughout the plant body

**pioneer community**—the living community that first colonizes bare ground or rock in the earliest stage of ecological succession

**pooter**—a piece of equipment used to collect fast-moving insects.

**producer**—a living organism, such as a plant, that uses inorganic materials to make its own food

**protozoan**—a minute organism found in marine, freshwater, and moist terrestrial habitats

**ray**—a cluster of horizontally oriented cells that radiate out from the center of a stem or trunk. They serve as horizontal pathways for the movement of food substances and water.

**relative humidity**—a measure of the actual amount of water vapor in the air relative to the maximum water vapor that the air could hold at a given temperature

**snag**—a dead, standing tree

**softwood**—the wood of coniferous trees such as pine and fir

**species diversity**—the variety and abundance of living forms, or species, in a defined area

**stoma** (pl. **stomata**)—a minute opening in the upper or lower cell layers of a leaf through which gases such as water vapor, carbon dioxide, and oxygen pass

**stratification**—the process of treating seeds to low temperatures for a period of time before attempting to germinate them

**succession**—the ordered progression of changing plant and animal communities that inhabit a site following its creation or a disturbance that wipes out previous communities

**symbiosis**—a close physical association between two individuals of different species

**topographic map**—a type of map that shows land features

**transpiration**—the loss of water vapor in a plant mostly through stomata

**understory**—a forest layer beneath the canopy; consisting of small trees and saplings

**vessel element**—an elongated cell found in the xylem of certain flowering plants, which transports water and dissolves minerals

**watershed**—an area of land that, by virtue of its shape and slope, funnels rain and snowmelt to a river, stream, lake, wetland, or ocean; all land areas on Earth are part of some watershed

**xylem**—a tissue found in most land plants that transports water and dissolved minerals throughout a plant and provides support for the plant body

# For Further Information

## Books

Berger, J. J. *Understanding Forests.* San Francisco, CA: Sierra Club Books, 1998.

Bland, J. B. *Forests of Lilliput: The Realm of Mosses and Lichens.* New Jersey: Prentice Hall, 1984.

Borror, D. J., and R. E. White. *A Field Guide to Insects, America North of Mexico.* Boston: Houghton Mifflin, 1970.

Burt, W. H., and R. P. Grossenheider. *A Field Guide to the Mammals,* 2nd ed. Boston: Houghton Mifflin, 1976.

Gardner, Robert. *Where on Earth Am I?* Danbury, CT: Franklin Watts, 1996.

Harlow, W. M. *Trees of the Eastern and Central United States and Canada.* New York: Dover Publications, 1957.

———. *Fruit Key and Twig Key to Trees and Shrubs.* New York: Dover Publications, 1946.

Hjellström, B. *Be Expert with Map and Compass.* New York: Macmillan, 1994.

Hutchins, R. E. *Galls and Gall Insects.* New York: Dodd, Mead & Company, 1969.

Kricher, J. C. *A Field Guide to California and Pacific Northwest Forests.* Boston: Houghton Mifflin, 1998.

———. *A Field Guide to Eastern Forests.* Boston: Houghton Mifflin, 1998.

———. *A Field Guide to Rocky Mountain and Southwestern Forests.* Boston: Houghton Mifflin, 1998.

Krieger, M. J. *Means & Probabilities: Using Statistics in Science Projects.* Danbury, CT: Franklin Watts, 1996.

Lewis, B. A. *The Kid's Guide to Social Action: How to Solve the Social Problems You Choose—And Turn Creative Thinking into Positive Action.* Minneapolis, MN: Free Spirit Publishing, 1991.

National Geographic Society. *Field Guide to the Birds of North America.* 2nd ed. Washington, DC: National Geographic Society, 1987.

Petrides, G. A. *A Field Guide to Trees and Shrubs.* Boston: Houghton Mifflin, 1972.

Sealander, J. A., and G. A. Heidt. *Arkansas Mammals: Their Natural History, Classification, and Distribution.* Fayetteville, AR: University of Arkansas Press, 1990.

## Videos

*Ancient Forests.* Washington, DC: National Geographic Society, 1992.

*Old Growth Forest: An Ecosystem.* Washington, DC: National Geographic Society, 1994.

*The Last Ancient Forests with James Redfield.* Washington, DC: Save America's Forests, 1998.

## Organizations and Online Sites

**Alaska Rainforest Campaign**
320 Fourth St. NE
Washington, DC 20002
*http://www.akrain.org*

**America Recycles Day**
*http://www.americarecyclesday.org*

**American Forests**
P.O. Box 2000
Washington, DC 20013-2000
*http://www.amfor.org*

**Co-op America, The Woodwise
Consumer Initiative**
1612 K St. NW, Suite 600
Washington, DC 20006
*http://www.woodwise.org*

**Environmental Monitoring and
Assessment Program**
*http://www.nbs.gov/nbii/emap.html*

**The National Arbor Day Foundation**
211 North 12th St.
Lincoln, NE 68508
*http://www.arborday.org*

**National Audubon Society**
Forest Campaign
1901 Pennsylvania Ave. NW, Suite 1100
Washington DC, 20006
*http://www.audubon.org*

**National Wildlife Federation**
1400 16th St. NW
Washington, DC 20036-2266

**Natural Resources Conservation Service**
*http://www.nrcs.usda.gov/*

**The Nature Conservancy**
1815 North Lynn St.
Arlington, VA 22209

**Save America's Forests**
4 Library Court SE
Washington, DC 20003
*http://saveamericasforests.org*

**Sierra Club**
85 2nd St., 2nd Floor
San Francisco, CA 94105
*http://www.sierraclub.org*

**Sierra Nevada Forest Protection Campaign**
*http://www.sierraforests.org*

**United States Environmental Protection Agency**
*http://www.epa.gov/surf*

**United States Fish and Wildlife Service**
*http://www.fws.gov/*

**United States Forest Service**
Public Affairs Office
14th St. and Independence Ave. SW
P.O. Box 96090
Washington, DC 20090-6090
*http://www.fs.fed.us/*

**United States Orienteering Federation**
*http://www.us.orienteering.org*

**The Wilderness Society**
900 17th St. NW
Washington, DC 20006-2596

## Equipment Suppliers

Abundant Life Seed Foundation
P.O. Box 772
Port Townsend, WA 98368
This nonprofit organization offers seeds for a number of
plants including trees.

American Forests, Famous and Historic Trees
8701 Old King's Rd.
Jacksonville, FL 32219
Seeds and seedlings of some trees are available through this program.

Carolina Biological Supply Company
2700 York Rd.
Burlington, NC 27215-3398
This company carries a wide variety of scientific tools and equipment as well as living and preserved specimens. Owl pellets can be purchased from them.

Educational Insights
16941 Keegan Ave.
Carson, CA 90746
This company sells educational materials and toys for kids. Among their many science supplies, they offer sun sensitive papers that can be developed in tap water. The trade name is Solargraphics.

Forestry Suppliers, Inc.
P.O. Box 8397
Jackson, MS 39284-8397
One of the major suppliers for forestry and environmental needs. Diameter tapes and devices to measure tree heights are available through this company.

J.L. Hudson, Seedsman
Star Route 2, Box 337
La Honda, CA 94020
Can be contacted by mail only. Offers seeds for a number of tree species.

LaMotte Company
P.O. Box 329
Chestertown, MD 21620
This company specializes in equipment and test kits for the analysis of water, soil, and air.

Pellets, Inc.
P.O. Box 5484
Bellingham, WA 98227-5484
This supplier offers barn owl pellets individually and as kits, along with charts and booklets to help you identify the skeletal remains found in the pellets.

WARD's
P.O. Box 92912
Rochester, NY 14692-9012
A science supply company that offers an inexpensive Imhoff cone.

United States Geological Survey (USGS),
Information Services
P.O. Box 25286
Denver Federal Center
Denver, CO 80255
You can obtain topographic maps from this agency for any area within the United States or Puerto Rico. To be able to specify which map or maps you will need, ask for their free index for any state.

# Index

# About the Author

Patricia A. Fink Martin brings to children's literature a professional biologist's breadth and depth of knowledge and an educator's enthusiasm and ability to communicate. She is a graduate of the University of Missouri. Continuing her training at Michigan State University, she received an M.S. in biochemistry. After teaching at a junior college for 2 years, she attended Idaho State University and completed a doctorate in the biological sciences with an emphasis on biology education.

Dr. Martin spent a number of years teaching college-level biochemistry, cell biology, anatomy, botany, zoology, and evolution. While teaching at a liberal arts college, she received a National Science Foundation award that allowed her to collaborate with a researcher at a nearby medical school.

While living in Florida, Dr. Martin tutored a home-schooled first-grader in science and participated in a national pen-pal program designed to bring young students in touch with a professional scientist. She now lives in Collierville, Tennessee, with her husband, Jerry, and their daughter, Leslie.

Dr. Martin's first book, *Animals that Walk on Water*, received a starred review in *Booklist* and was listed among the top ten children's animal books for 1998. *Woods and Forests* is her ninth book. She has written one other book in the Exploring Ecosystems series.